Praise for
There Is More

'Brian Houston is a dear friend who knows what God can do in your life when you surrender all. *There Is More* will help you learn to live a fulfilled life by trusting God to take control. I challenge you to allow this book to impact your life.'

— RICK WARREN, senior pastor of Saddleback Church

'If you've ever felt that you've been created for something greater, pastor Brian Houston's new book, *There Is More,* is exactly what you need. Packed with spiritual truth, deep insights, and practical wisdom, this book reveals how your future can hold more than you ever thought possible. Read *There Is More* and prepare for God to build your faith, stretch your mind, and enlarge your perspective of what He wants to do through you.'

— CRAIG GROESCHEL, pastor of Life.Church and author of
Divine Direction: 7 Decisions That Will Change Your Life

'Why is it that most of us have what we need yet still find ourselves striving for more? My friend Brian Houston taps into this dichotomy and challenges us in the way that only he can. If you'll dig into this book, I'm confident you'll walk away with a greater expectation for your future.'

— STEVEN FURTICK, pastor of Elevation Church and *New York Times* best-selling author

'There couldn't be a more timely or needed book. In these confusing days, we need to be stretched where our thinking is limited, expanded where our dreams are small, and reminded that our God is not a God of confusion. In Brian Houston's *There Is More,* we are encouraged to hold tight to that truth, believing that His peace, power, and light abound in even the darkest of times and that through us He can and will do immeasurably more than we can ever imagine.'

—ROMA DOWNEY, actor, producer, and president
of LightWorkers Media

'Brian Houston is an exceptional leader—God loving, Jesus focused, Holy Spirit anointed, authentic, credible, and pioneering. *There Is More* is a treasure trove of inspiring visionary teaching and leadership insights, combined with fascinating anecdotes and his own powerful testimony. I hope you will enjoy this book as much as I did.'

—NICKY GUMBEL, vicar of HTB Church, London

'Brian's approach in explaining how to seek God, walk by faith, dream big, and trust Him completely is very effective. I believe many will experience more of God's destiny in their lives through the inspiration he shares.'

—JOYCE MEYER, Bible teacher and best-selling author

'I respect and admire Pastor Brian so much that when my own dad and pastor was valiantly fighting cancer, it felt only natural to me that Pastor Brian was the kind of father, husband, and pastor I could look to for leadership in these next seasons of my life. I literally began to call him 'my pastor,' and the rest, as they say, is history. When I read *There Is More,* I noticed that the character of God has spurred Pastor Brian on to desire more of Him, to learn more about Him, to follow His hand with great faith, and to live with an expectation of His goodness in all circumstances. This hunger for more is sincere and deep and very real; not for things but for a vibrant relationship with his God. Not because he is a pastor, or a husband, or a father, but because he is first a follower of Jesus. It's clear from these pages that Pastor Brian actively cultivates this beautiful appetite for more of God. And now he whets all of our appetites as well.'

—JUDAH SMITH, lead pastor of Churchome.org and best-selling author of *Jesus Is* _____.

'God has a plan and a purpose for your life that is bigger than you. But God needs you to believe it, know what's inside of you to achieve it, and build the character that sustains it. Brian Houston's new book, *There Is More,* will show you the way! Don't just make it a part of your library; make it a part of your life!'

—A. R. BERNARD, ambassador for Christ in Culture

'My friend Pastor Brian is a strong man of God and a phenomenal leader to the body of Christ. His new book, *There Is More,* will challenge you to pursue the calling God has given you with renewed passion and fervor. This book is an invitation for God to take you beyond what you dreamed to be possible!'

—JOHN BEVERE, author and minister, Messenger International

THERE IS MORE

WHEN THE WORLD SAYS YOU CAN'T,
GOD SAYS YOU CAN

BRIAN HOUSTON

WILLIAM
COLLINS

William Collins
An imprint of HarperCollins*Publishers*
1 London Bridge Street
London SE1 9GF

WilliamCollinsBooks.com

First published in Great Britain in 2018 by William Collins

This edition published by arrangement with WaterBrook Press, an imprint of the Crown Publishing Group, a division of Penguin Random House LLC

4

To the wonderful people who have loved me through the highs and lows of my best and worst seasons, none more so than Bobbie and our beautiful extended family, thank you for doing the journey.

To the long-serving board and elders of Hillsong Church, you have led the way and faithfully stood alongside us, always seeking the will of God. I am eternally grateful to each and every one of you.

And to the team who have worked closest to Bobbie and me through all these years, who have always wanted only God's best for us and spurred us on toward the "more" of God's ever-unfolding purposes, you have my deepest respect and appreciation.

CONTENTS

Introduction

Exceeding, Abundant, and Above

Please, sir, I want some more."[*] These famous words of a starving Oliver Twist have undoubtedly echoed in the hearts and minds of millions of people who also long to have just a little bit more. Perhaps you long for more time, more resources, more space. Maybe you simply need to find a bit more energy and motivation to continue along the path you currently find yourself on, or maybe you have a dream in your heart that continues to evade you. Maybe you're walking in your calling but still find yourself asking, *What is this all about? Should I be doing more with my life?*

The narrative of this book is not about selfishness and greed. It's not about acquiring more, about avarice and indulgence. It's not even an essay on satisfaction and self-fulfillment. It's about calling—God's amazing plans for your life and the sufficiency of His grace in superseding your wildest dreams, all for a purpose bigger than you are.

Have you ever stopped to wonder what God's response would be to

---

[*] Charles Dickens, *Oliver Twist*, in *Works of Charles Dickens, Household Edition* (New York: Sheldon, 1864), 34.

your heart's cry for more? It is my firm belief that, unlike Mr. Bumble (the tyrannical caretaker of the orphanage in Charles Dickens's classic novel), the Savior of the universe would bend down and in the most caring of manners say, "More what? And how much more? My supply is unending. My mercy is limitless. My grace is more than you need."

You see, the more that God wants for your life is beyond comprehension. It's not limited to space and time, not able to be measured with earthly devices or human minds. Ephesians 3:20–21 tells us plainly, "God can do anything, you know—far more than you could ever imagine or guess or request in your wildest dreams! He does it not by pushing us around but by working within us, his Spirit deeply and gently within us" (MSG). Other translations put it this way: He can "do above and beyond" (HCSB) or "exceedingly abundantly above all that we ask or think."

Have you ever stopped to think about that? God can do *anything*. And not just a little bit more than you have already asked for or dreamed of. *Far* more.

What are your wildest dreams? Your craziest ideas, deepest longings, and grandest plans—the things you've not dared tell anyone and barely allowed your soul to imagine? Because it is exactly that dream, that vision, those grand plans of yours that I'm telling you aren't enough. What a small thinker you are! All of heaven is looking down upon you, shaking their heads, and saying, "Is that *all*?! Is that all he wants? Is that all she can dream of?"

Allow me to stretch your thinking here, dear reader, because we serve the ultimate Big Thinker. No plans of yours even *compare* to His. Your heart's cry for more has been answered with a chuckle and a grin from a Father's heart that takes what you see and expands it into something you can't see.

God can take every limitation that has been put on your life—by yourself or by others—and expand your heart and purpose in a way that is *way* bigger, *way* higher, *way* more effective than anything you could imagine.

I've seen it in my own life. I can testify to His faithfulness when it comes to more—more than I wanted, more than I dreamed, more than I ever thought I would need. I'm not speaking of simple material matters, of monetary things or things that can be counted or valued by earthly standards. I've watched as God has exceeded the dreams in my heart, the visions I've had for my own life and the lives of my family and those closest to me. I've experienced the "much more" favor of God when it comes to my marriage, leadership, children, and friendships.

For many years, while standing in one of our Hillsong Church auditoriums or by the side of the stage at one of our annual conferences, people have asked me, "Could you see all this when you started?" You know, I have always been a determined visionary, but in my wildest dreams I could not have imagined all God has done and is doing. I couldn't have planned it, executed it, or dreamed of the days we are living in now. And I've stopped trying to. You can never out-dream God.

I've learned to trust God with the secret desires of my heart—the things I don't know that I need and the things I thought I didn't need. Many a time, I've discovered there is more to the valleys I walked through than simply the pain I experienced. There is more to learn in storms than what my eyes were fixed on in the natural. There is more purpose to my provision than simply my own fulfillment and enjoyment—so much more.

In fact, in the sentences preceding the glorious verse I already quoted (Ephesians 3:20–21), we are given a glimpse into the reason for our more:

I bow my knees to the Father of our Lord Jesus Christ, from whom the whole family in heaven and earth is named, that He would grant you, according to the riches of His glory, to be strengthened with might through His Spirit in the inner man, that Christ may dwell in your hearts through faith; that you, being rooted and grounded in love, may be able to comprehend with all the saints what is the width and length and depth and height—to know the love of Christ which passes knowledge; that you may be filled with all the fullness of God.

Now to Him who is able to do exceedingly abundantly above all that we ask or think, according to the power that works in us, to Him be glory in the church by Christ Jesus to all generations, forever and ever. Amen. (verses 14–21)

Filled with all the fullness of God. Glory to all generations.

This book is about exactly that: the character and nature of the God we serve and His desire to see each and every one of us experience that Ephesians 3 life—His desire to see us filled to overflowing with every good, wonderful, and perfect gift from Him, purposed to build the church, expand the kingdom, and echo His name throughout the generations. The following chapters unfold the purpose of our more, the source of our more, and the understanding that <u>more</u> is less <u>about us</u>, <u>more about others</u>, and <u>all about Him</u>. But first you need to understand that our heavenly Father sees more in you than you could ever see in yourself.

My prayer is that you will turn each of these pages and discover something new within the ancient text scattered throughout. I hope that regardless of the prayers you have prayed, the triumphs you've celebrated, the failures you've lived or perceived, you will come to understand that there is more grace, goodness, mercy, kindness, love, forgiveness, and favor waiting in your future. God's will for your life—heaven's perfect purpose—is indeed beyond your wildest dreams. And if you have ever asked for more and, like Oliver Twist, been met by angry words or an indifferent spirit, or if you've ever had your motives questioned or been unjustly assailed, I pray that through my personal experiences and revelation, you will find healing as you discover a little bit more about the true character of our giving God and His desires for my life.

There is always more to uncover—more to discover about who He is and who He says you are. There is more ahead of you than you've allowed yourself to dream or allowed yourself to believe. There is more room in your life for the things of God and the people of God than you even thought possible—more space to be made for God to make His presence known in and through you. And if for some reason you've stopped dreaming big things for your life, stopped imagining that your life is a story to tell or a legacy to be remembered, then this book is a good place to start again.

1

Dreams and Destiny

Seventeen. What did you dream about when you were seventeen? Did you dare to dream? Were you allowed to dream? Were you laughed at for your dreams? Perhaps family or peers were threatened by your dreams. Or are you the product of an environment where you were encouraged to think big and dream impossible dreams? And if you are not yet seventeen or are well beyond seventeen, what grand things do you dream about now?

I was a dreamer. You see, I came from a land that was then said to have three million people and seventy million sheep. That's great if your life's grand ambition is making woolen jumpers or Roquefort cheese, but it's not necessarily a launching pad for dreaming of building anything with worldwide influence and impact. Interestingly, this small land in the Southern Ocean has produced (among many other fine endeavors) the first man to climb Mount Everest and the first man to split the atom. It is home to the famous landscape displayed in the splendor of the Lord of the Rings movies, as well as many world-renowned entertainers, actors, athletes, and businesspeople. Plus of course it boasts the world's most successful and famed rugby team, the New Zealand All Blacks. So maybe, just maybe, humble beginnings are the perfect soil for a blossoming and fruitful life.

In the 1960s, my family lived in a state house, which was a government-owned, timber-lined dwelling that stood like a sullen soldier among all the other similar houses in Taita, Lower Hutt, New Zealand. It was a working-class suburb, with all the associated social problems, just outside Wellington.

Nothing in particular stood out about me as a child or teenager. I found it impossible to concentrate in school, and my long legs were more of a hindrance than a help when it came to the sporting field.

I have vivid memories of my journey home from Hutt Valley High School. I began my daily walk from the train station onto High Street before turning left past the Tocker Street Dairy, our local convenience store, where, if I had any change, I would stop to buy hokey-pokey ice cream (vanilla ice cream with small bits of honeycomb toffee throughout). Then I would veer right onto Reynolds Street, past Pearce Crescent, Molesworth Street, and Compton Crescent, before finally turning into Nash Street, and I would walk past three houses before arriving home at the corner of Nash Street and Taita Drive. And day after day, on that repetitious walk home, my young, shy, but adventurous mind used to dream and dream and dream. It was a dream that always seemed to follow a similar narrative.

For as long as I can remember, I wanted to someday serve Jesus and preach the gospel. In fact, I cannot remember a time when that wasn't what I dreamed of doing. I dreamed in the school classroom, I dreamed on that journey home, and I dreamed while sitting in church twice on a Sunday, every Sunday throughout my childhood.

It was then that I imagined speaking to big crowds or traveling the world, leading thousands of people to Jesus Christ and maybe one day building a great church. I would also wonder who my wife would be, what she would look like, where she was, and what she was doing at that very moment. And I dreamed that maybe I would meet her—that one person who would want to pursue this dream with me.

Fast-forward forty-plus years, and I have found myself on a much longer journey than that childhood walk home from the train station. It's been this ongoing adventure called life, in which this small-town daydreamer has found himself living in the realization of those dreams and in the wonder of even bigger ones.

Dare to Dream

As I mentioned, concentration was never my strong point. I distinctly remember that the comments of my schoolteachers followed a theme: "Brian doesn't listen"; "Brian could do so much better if he didn't daydream"; "Brian procrastinates."

In the 1960s, our church congregation was about five hundred to six hundred people. At the time, it was possibly the largest church in the country, but it was still not an especially large group. Looking back now, I realize that if I had shared my wide-eyed, wonderful, and global dreams out loud, many would have politely laughed or perhaps shared a patronizing smile with other adults nearby. For a young pastor's son from a low-income neighborhood in an astoundingly beautiful land of millions of sheep, what outrageous dreams they were! Although I never got the feeling that anyone had high expectations about my future, I just kept on dreaming anyway.

When I was seventeen years old, I held eleven different jobs to raise enough money to go to Bible college. That's too many jobs to name, but not one of them was my passion. Yet I worked hard because I was preparing and planning for the things I was passionate about. So, despite the odds against me and the jobs I didn't want, I never lost sight of the dreams in my heart.

I believe that the ability to dream is one of God's greatest gifts. So let me ask you again, what do you dream about? Do you dream of things far bigger than you are? I believe it was those wild dreams of mine as a boy that led me to Bible college and set me on the path I find myself on today.

The Bigger the Better

Have you ever heard the saying "If you aim at nothing, you'll hit it every time"? Well, in the same way, if you aim at a target, you might not hit the bull's-eye, but at least you'll get as close as you can. Even if your dreams become only 80 percent real, it's still better than nothing at all!

The truth is, you *should* shoot for the moon. God gave you the ability to dream, to create, and to imagine endless possibilities. In many ways, dreaming is just like faith, and the size of your dream can be in direct correlation to your belief in what God can achieve. In my opinion, if you're dreaming about something you can do on your own, you're dreaming too small! God-sized dreams are dreams that can be done only when you put your faith in the Creator, the One who knows the beginning from the end and who desires your future to be filled with hope and abundance. So much potential perishes because of the lack of an audacious dream.

So, what did your life look like when you were seventeen? What was it that made you drift off from the present and dream about the future?

Are you still dreaming now? Perhaps you didn't dream of anything outrageous or were never prone to believe for something outside your current reality, but I believe that everyone should have a dream—a dream bigger than he is and one that is impossible to fulfill in an individual's own strength. Dreams come in varied forms. You can consciously dream by having aspirations for your future, and you can physically dream through visions in your sleep. I believe that God can work through and speak to us in both ways. Dreaming is important, as your dreams can become your destiny. So if you don't have a dream, you are limiting your destiny.

I dare you to dream big, scary, and outrageous dreams—the kind that would make other people laugh if only they knew. The Bible tells us about a seventeen-year-old dreamer exactly like that. This young man dreamed an outrageous dream, and for him, that dream was only the beginning.

The Sun, the Moon, and the Stars

The young dreamer I'm talking about is, of course, Joseph. Here is the story of his dream:

> Joseph, being seventeen years old, was pasturing the flock with his
> brothers. He was a boy with the sons of Bilhah and Zilpah, his
> father's wives. And Joseph brought a bad report of them to their
> father. Now Israel loved Joseph more than any other of his sons,
> because he was the son of his old age. And he made him a robe
> of many colors. But when his brothers saw that their father loved
> him more than all his brothers, they hated him and could not
> speak peacefully to him.

Now Joseph had a dream, and when he told it to his brothers they hated him even more. He said to them, "Hear this dream that I have dreamed: Behold, we were binding sheaves in the field, and behold, my sheaf arose and stood upright. And behold, your sheaves gathered around it and bowed down to my sheaf." His brothers said to him, "Are you indeed to reign over us? Or are you indeed to rule over us?" So they hated him even more for his dreams and for his words.

Then he dreamed another dream and told it to his brothers and said, "Behold, I have dreamed another dream. Behold, the sun, the moon, and eleven stars were bowing down to me." But when he told it to his father and to his brothers, his father rebuked him and said to him, "What is this dream that you have dreamed? Shall I and your mother and your brothers indeed come to bow ourselves to the ground before you?" And his brothers were jealous of him, but his father kept the saying in mind." (Genesis 37:1–11, ESV)

Sheaves of grain bowing down to him, and even the sun, the moon, and the stars! From where Joseph sat, tending sheep in the land of Canaan, his dreams looked absurd. Talk about shooting for the moon—he imagined that even the moon would be within his grasp!

When I dreamed as a child about traveling to places I had learned about in school, there was nothing in the natural that made these dreams look possible. I would take a pen and doodle on the back of my schoolbooks pictures of such places as Paris, with its outdoor cafés, poodles, and endless baguettes. I dreamed about London, with its unique black cabs, double-decker buses, and destinations I knew from our family Monopoly board, such as Fleet Street, Coventry Street, Park Lane, and Mayfair. And I was always fascinated by bigger places, such as Australia or other countries that then seemed so far away. The United States of America and everything it offered seemed like another world back then. Today those dreams have become so much a part of my life that I hardly think about the fact that they were once a dream.

How often do you believe for the impossible?

About twenty years ago, I spent an afternoon in my office with a blank piece of paper in front of me and wrote down the words "The Church That I See." Quite miraculously, the amazing thing is that thirty years on, in many ways, those words I wrote down are reflective of the church we now lead. But it wasn't always that way.

In 1983, Hillsong Church was a gathering of less than one hundred people in a tiny school hall. It was a passionate, vibrant, young community of believers, along with a few almost believers and even nonbelievers, putting out chairs, sweeping the floor, and praying in a broom closet before and after services each Sunday. The "stage" was a road case, and the quality of the band was modest at best. Hillsong Church looks very different now, but many of the values that we built on are the same today.

Hillsong has always been a worshipping church. Before there was Hillsong UNITED, before there was Hillsong Young & Free, before there was "Shout to the Lord," "Mighty to Save," or "Oceans," there was worship. Passionate worship. It wasn't always polished, there weren't always lights, and in those early years, there wasn't even a stage, but we worshipped. We sang and we began to take baby steps in writing songs that resounded in the hearts of the people in our community. Sure, the piano had one or two notes that didn't work and was out of tune, and the drummer didn't keep a steady beat. Jack, our smiling senior accordion player and his wife, Elaine, not only were a part of the band but also looked after the tiny group of kids in our children's ministry, including our own four-year-old and eighteen-month-old sons. Those were rough, raw, pioneering days, but the fruit of the labor of many faithful people early on began to give way to opportunities beyond our wildest dreams.

It was on that piece of paper, more than two decades ago, that I wrote these words: "I see a church whose heartfelt praise and worship touches heaven and changes earth—worship that influences the praises of people throughout the earth, exalting Christ with powerful songs of faith and hope."

Only one year before I wrote that, in 1992, the very first live Hillsong album was released: *The Power of Your Love.* But even before that, we recorded our first musical effort, *Spirit and Truth,* in a tiny home studio. I was so proud of that little collection of original songs that, when I had the chance as a pastor to speak at a citywide gathering of hundreds of ministers (almost all older, wiser, and more seasoned than I was), I made them first listen to some of the songs. I can still see the blank stares sending a clear message that no one in the room was anywhere near as excited about this as I was. But the idea of recording an album simply came from our passion to worship God in our local church, along with the belief that our local church was called to resource other local churches with words and music that would glorify our worthy God. At the time, we never could have imagined that our albums would be sung throughout the earth, but we had a belief that God had called us to do something with what was in our hands and that, as we were faithful, He would also be faithful.

Now, more than ninety albums later, God is growing and stretching and changing the story of Hillsong Worship. But it was long before those first albums that the songs of God and the sound of our house were established as a priority, an arrowhead, and a cornerstone of who we are—all because of a God-breathed dream.

The Bible tells us in Zechariah 4:10, "Do not despise these small beginnings" (NLT). Whatever it is God has entrusted into your hand—your family, your career, your ministry, or whatever—don't count it as insignificant. Whatever dreams are in your heart and still seem like a world away, don't be discouraged! I believe that in the eyes of God and with His leading, wisdom, favor, and provision, if you hold fast to that dream He has placed in your heart, you, like Joseph, will see it come to pass.

Dream Killers

Among the youngest of the sons in his family, Joseph probably took his fair share of mocking and rough-ups from his older brothers. Yet when Joseph dreamed of his mother, father, and brothers bowing down to him, he didn't hesitate to share with them the God-sized dream. It had the predictable effect: it enraged his family.

Joseph's brothers waited for their chance to get back at him. When they were out with the flocks one time and Joseph came to them, they knew their chance had come. "They saw him in the distance, and before he had reached them, they plotted to kill him. They said to one another, 'Here comes that dreamer! Come on, let's kill him and throw him into one of the pits. We can say that a vicious animal ate him. Then we'll see what becomes of his dreams!" (Genesis 37:18–20, HCSB).

Because of Joseph's dream, his brothers tried to kill him. He was captured, thrown in a pit, and sold into slavery. Talk about dream killers!

But Joseph didn't stop dreaming.

Have you ever had a dream die? Have you ever shared your dream with anyone? Perhaps you have and you've been mocked for it. Maybe when you finally opened your mouth to share about the impossible longings in your heart, you were met with laughter or cynicism or hurt by the words spoken to you by the people you love.

Dreaming can be a lonely place. If you're going to dream things that will set you apart, sometimes the people who are closest to you and know you best will be the very ones who are threatened by the trajectory of your life and will oppose you, try to squash your dreams, and bring you down to size. So, if you are going to be a dreamer, understand that it can be a lonely road. You are going to need to hold fast to your convictions and hold firm to the Word of God and the desires of your heart, despite the criticism or accolades you receive along the way.

What it comes down to is that you have an enemy who would love to kill your dream with all sorts of "realities," such as opposition or lack of resources. Often the negative voices of other people, or even the wrong ambition in your own heart, can suffocate your dreams. Sometimes along the path toward your dreams, you have to make choices and sacrifices that feel like backward movement instead of forward motion.

When I married Bobbie, I told her, "Sweetheart, we might never own our own home or have a new car or a lot of money, but we will serve Jesus together." For the first year of our marriage, to be volunteer youth pastors in a small suburban church in South Auckland (near where Bobbie grew up), we both worked multiple jobs. Bobbie was a secretary in a pharmaceutical company, and I was in sales. I had after-hours jobs cleaning the bathrooms in an automobile factory and stocking shelves in a supermarket—all because we were passionate to serve God. And we desired to, when the time was right, build a local church that was enjoyable and warm and filled with people who were influential in their own spheres. In many ways it wasn't easy as we gave our all in the local church, but it was the very sacrifices that we made then that enabled us to keep dreaming now, confident in a God who always provides. We could have let the setbacks take us off course, but we held fast to the vision we had for our lives.

I don't know about you, but I don't want to just live on a dream I had way back in the past. I want to keep dreaming new dreams. Being a dreamer isn't past tense; it is an ongoing part of life! Just like Joseph of old, dreamers never stop dreaming. Despite the obstacles put in front of them, the limitations imposed on them, or the dream killers that get in the way, dreamers just keep on dreaming!

Surrounded by Dreamers

In order to keep dreaming, you need to surround yourself with other dreamers. Find people who will walk alongside you and remind you of your dream when setbacks make you want to forget. Keep company with people who inspire you to dream and breathe encouragement into your vision—people who will keep you on course.

Winston Churchill, the Nobel Prize–winning, twice-elected wartime prime minster of the United Kingdom, wasn't always as well regarded as he is today. In fact, he struggled in school and failed the sixth grade. Later, he faced many years of political failures until he finally became the prime minister at the ripe old age of sixty-five. Churchill was a dreamer—he dreamed of making a difference in his nation. And when he finally got elected to office, he credited his wife of almost thirty-two years for continuously dreaming along with him and believing in him, despite his failures and the financial hardship and public ridicule they endured. Clementine Churchill is not often spoken of, but history may never have recorded her husband's achievements without her support of his dreams.

Who is cheering you on? Who is offering you consolation in the form of encouragement while your dreams are yet to be realized?

Being around other dreamers is a catalyst for dreaming bigger. Proverbs 29:18 says, "Where there is no vision, the people perish" (KJV) or "cast off restraint" (NIVII). The New Living Translation says they "run wild." The Message translates it like this:

> If people can't see what God is doing,
>   they stumble all over themselves;
> But when they attend to what he reveals,
>   they are most blessed.

A dream will indeed cause you to sacrifice and make the hard choices, but perhaps more importantly, it will also cause you to choose your friends wisely. Who are you dreaming alongside?

Determined to Succeed

Nobody begins to pursue a dream believing that it will fail. Sounds simple, right? But a lot of people don't necessarily dream to succeed; they dream to function and survive but don't dream of success, perhaps because it feels too indulgent.

Let me assure you there is nothing wrong with success. The God who wants to give you abundantly above all you could ask or think is the same God who wants to see you succeed!

Joseph's dream was a dream of success, and it came to pass. Years after Joseph's brothers sold him into slavery in Egypt, this happened:

Pharaoh said to Joseph, ". . . You shall be over my house, and all my people shall be ruled according to your word; only in regard to the throne will I be greater than you." And Pharaoh said to Joseph, "See, I have set you over all the land of Egypt."

Then Pharaoh took his signet ring off his hand and put it on Joseph's hand; and he clothed him in garments of fine linen and put a gold chain around his neck. And he had him ride in the second chariot which he had; and they cried out before him, "Bow the knee!" So he set him over all the land of Egypt. (Genesis 41:39–43)

God isn't going to give you a dream of mediocrity. Believe it or not, *success* is a biblical word! See what the Lord said to Joshua when he took charge of the nation of Israel:

Only be strong and very courageous, that you may observe to do according to all the law which Moses My servant commanded you; do not turn from it to the right hand or to the left, that you may prosper wherever you go. This Book of the Law shall not depart from your mouth, but you shall meditate in it day and night, that you may observe to do according to all that is written in it. For then you will make your way prosperous, and then you will have good success. (Joshua 1:7–8)

Good success.

Define success however you like, but the way God defines it is different than the way the world does. It's not about acquisition or self-indulgence. Success in the kingdom of God is so often about service.

[handwritten: darkness to others Be set FREE]

Good Success Versus Bad Success

Most people have the will to *live;* fewer people have the will to *succeed,* because of the personal cost involved; still fewer people have the will to *serve.* The point of serving God is that we live to succeed and we succeed to serve. *[handwritten: I need to have something to share to help/serve people]*

When you live with a dream in your heart and with humility to serve, you *really* live. When your dreams and your success are centered on serving the cause of Christ and those around you, you become part of the 1 percent. Who is the 1 percent? The group of once-in-a-generation type of leaders who cause others to sit up and take notice. The people who, regardless of their inhibitions and limitations, are determined to live out their dreams and fulfill their destinies. People who believe deep down that they are called to do something important with their lives.

Have you ever been camping? In an arid and sunburned country like Australia, sleeping under the stars means getting well acquainted with the dust of the ground. Life can be like that. Looking up at the sky, we can dream great things. It's like setting out on a camping trip, imagining the beautiful starry nights, sleeping by a campfire, roasting marshmallows, and grilling your freshly caught fish. But the realities of living out that experience also mean we must find the tent, pack the car, drive to the destination, pitch the tent, sweep out the dirt, swat the flies, spray the bug repellent, and manage without the conveniences of home—all so we position ourselves to experience that dream. Then when the dream becomes real and we are enjoying the magnificent starry night, it seems all the sweeter because the value of our sacrifice and diligence is now in perspective. "Oh, this was *so* worth it!"

So what happens when ordinary people begin to serve—to live their lives with a purpose in mind and focus on making it happen? The dust of the ground is the domain of servants, while the stars of the sky are the realms of kings. When we have servant hearts, it makes us perfect fits for greatness and impossibilities realized, for blessings promised and for the Word of God to work in our lives.

Jesus said, "Whoever desires to become great among you, let him be your servant. And whoever desires to be first among you, let him be your slave—just as the Son of Man did not come to be served, but to serve, and to give His life a ransom for many" (Matthew 20:26–28).

We should never underestimate what God can do with the dreams in our hearts and the dust of the ground. I don't know what we'd do with a rib—maybe cook it up or give it to the dog—but God took a rib and made something of exquisite beauty: woman (see Genesis 2:22). He began with the dust, but He didn't leave things there. We serve an amazing God!

If you have a dream in your heart, then you need to be a sower. A sower works the ground, and the process of sowing and reaping is a principle of the ground. Reaping what you sow is not just an Old Testament idea or a New Testament idea; it's an eternal principle, a biblical promise. If you sow in good ground, you will reap a harvest. In other words, what will get you to your dream—what you sow—is what will keep your dream thriving. Essentially, servants live for something far greater than themselves. Servants understand the value of their contribution in building something great.

Many years ago, when my television ministry was a very simple setup in a makeshift studio out behind one of our office buildings, a young boy used to volunteer each week to make coffee, run errands, and serve the producer and small crew of people who made it happen. When he was just fourteen years of age, his mum would drop him off each week, and with a pure heart and a spirit to learn, he simply hung around the studios taking in the wonder of film and television and doing whatever was needed, no matter how big or small.

Ten years into the future, and the dream in this boy's heart began to take shape as his talents made a way for him onto the set, and eventually he became the director of one of Australia's longest-running and most-watched television series. It was on the set of this show that he met his wife, one of the lead actresses in the program and also a believer in Christ. However, it was never his aspiration to climb the ladder of corporate success in Hollywood. He always kept a secret longing in his heart to attach his obvious talents to the kingdom of God, and wherever possible he continued to serve the vision of Hillsong through consultation and volunteering.

Today Ben Field is the head of our entire Hillsong film and television department and the creative genius behind all the content on Hillsong Channel. Week in and week out, he manages a growing staff of producers, directors, production teams, writers, and editors who are creating cutting-edge media for our church and global audiences. His passion for the church, willingness to serve, and expertise in his field have set him up to be a great blessing to Bobbie and me and to take us forward in the world of television and other media in a way we never imagined.

Impossibilities are made possible through our daily choices.

The Word of God says it plainly: if you want to be great, serve. It's how Jesus ministered on earth, with service being the quality that set Him apart from all others. Never underestimate the power of servant leadership. Remember, in the kingdom of God, the way up is down. The road to reaching the lofty heights of our dreams and visions for the future begins on the dusty ground of servanthood. And the act of becoming a servant will move you from the ordinary to the extraordinary.

Your dreams are nothing compared to God's dreams for you. There is more to your life than what you can even imagine, so why not dare to dream big?

The Bible goes on to tell us that not only did Joseph's dreams come to fruition, but his unexpected position and power in Egypt brought safety and care to his family and the nation. Your destiny is abundantly above all you could ask or imagine; your success, much like Joseph's, was planned and dreamed for even before the foundations of the earth. Just as Joseph's destiny ultimately took him to a place of great influence and authority, so too can your future bring blessing into your life and positively affect the lives of those around you. For us as believers, our success is never just for ourselves, and so often it simply starts with a dream.

2

Myth or Mystery?

We do not know this Australian's name and we never will.
We do not know his rank or his battalion. We do not know
where he was born, nor precisely how and when he died.
We do not know where in Australia he had made his home
or when he left it for the battlefields of Europe. We do not
know his age or his circumstances—whether he was from
the city or the bush; what occupation he left to become a
soldier; what religion, if he had a religion; if he was married
or single. We do not know who loved him or whom he
loved. If he had children we do not know who they are. His
family is lost to us as he was lost to them. We will never
know who this Australian was.

—PAUL KEATING, "Remembrance Day 1993:
Commemorative Address"

Similar to other countries, Australia has a Tomb of the Unknown
Soldier, located in Canberra. The mystery that surrounds the story
of the unknown Australian soldier has captured the imagination of a nation. It tells of an unknown yet brave man who valiantly fought for his

country and was wounded beyond recognition, leaving history to write his story.

Mystery, indeed, has intrigued the human soul for as long as time. Humanity's intrepid nature has caused hundreds of explorers to conquer mountains that others said couldn't be climbed. We are enamored with stories of the outer universe—places we have never been and never even seen. Human hearts have longed to travel farther than their imaginations will even allow. Tales of buried treasure and mysterious disappearances spark excitement in the minds of children; the great unknown draws people in like moths to a flame.

When I was a child, it was this penchant to understand that which wasn't explained that often got me in trouble. "Don't touch that hot plate, Brian." "Stay Back, Wet Paint." Warnings such as these were magnets for my curious personality. To this day, when food is delivered to my table with the warning "Be very careful—the plate is hot," curiosity still sparks a compulsion for me to find out just how hot.

We are drawn to explain that which has no explanation.

It is natural, therefore, to be intrigued with the beauty and wonder of the vastness and mysterious nature of who God is. Our human understanding tries to reason Him into a rational and manageable size. Theologians try to explain Him and answer questions that continue to be asked time after time. Yet God remains far beyond human understanding. We cannot manage Him or fit Him into our realm of comprehension. We cannot restrict Him by our limited notions of what is possible. We want answers to questions that were meant to lead only to more questions. God is complex and ambiguous yet simple and clear.

Daring to dream big causes us to ask questions such as "What does God want for my life?" "How does God fit into this plan, or this plan into God's?" "Does an infinite God even care about the finite details?" "Why did that roadblock stop me in my tracks?" and "Why does that person always seem to have more, while others have less?"

The Mystery of the Kingdom

In our quest to discover more of who we are and more of who God is, it is natural that we will come up against the unknown—the mysterious and often unanswerable. Even the apostle Paul referred to the mystery of Christ twenty-one times in his epistles. But perhaps it was Job who said it best when he wrote,

> Do you think you can explain the mystery of God?
>   Do you think you can diagram God Almighty?
> God is far higher than you can imagine,
>   far deeper than you can comprehend,
> Stretching farther than earth's horizons,
>   far wider than the endless ocean. (Job 11:7–9, MSG)

Jesus often used parables to peel back the great mysteries of the kingdom of God. He started almost all His stories with "The kingdom of God is like . . ." or "The kingdom of heaven is like . . ." and then went on to expound truth to listening crowds. These parables are simple, enabling us to relate the gospel to our everyday lives, even today, by talking of farming and fishing, vineyards and seed sowing. Yet they are also profound and layered with wonderful mysteries. We can find varying interpretations of every single one online at the click of a button.

Life with Jesus is filled with possibilities, and when we enter into relationship with Him, we enter into a world of wonderful secrets and revealed truth, especially when it comes to things beyond human understanding.

The statement "There is more" could not be truer about anything than that which we experience in the Christian life. There is more to know, there is more to understand, and there is more to come. The more we know about God and His Word, the more we realize we don't yet know. Layer after layer, mystery after mystery, treasure after treasure, indeed more after more is revealed to us when seeking Him is our prize.

The Mystery of God's Will

It was three o'clock in the morning. In the pitch black of night, the men peered over the side of the boat they were sailing in and saw a mysterious figure moving toward them across the water. Was it a ghost? What could this frightening encounter be? They had just finished ministering to a crowd of thousands earlier that day and were crossing the Sea of Galilee:

> Now in the fourth watch of the night Jesus went to them, walk-
> ing on the sea. And when the disciples saw Him walking on the
> sea, they were troubled, saying, "It is a ghost!" And they cried out
> for fear.
>
> But immediately Jesus spoke to them, saying, "Be of good
> cheer! It is I; do not be afraid."
>
> And Peter answered Him and said, "Lord, if it is You,
> command me to come to You on the water."
>
> So He said, "Come." And when Peter had come down out
> of the boat, he walked on the water to go to Jesus. But when he

saw that the wind was boisterous, he was afraid; and beginning
to sink he cried out, saying, "Lord, save me!"

And immediately Jesus stretched out His hand and caught
him, and said to him, "O you of little faith, why did you doubt?"
And when they got into the boat, the wind ceased.

Then those who were in the boat came and worshiped Him,
saying, "Truly You are the Son of God." (Matthew 14:25–33)

Let me tell you, just as the disciples discovered, there is so much in-
trigue, mystery, and suspense when you choose to follow Christ. Maybe
you are asking the same question Peter asked: "God, is that really You?"
Perhaps you are wondering what is next for you on your faith journey. Or
you may be asking the question that seems to pop into every believer's
head at least once a year: *What is the will of God for my life?* Well, I've
got news for you. Sometimes to discover the mystery of what is next—
the mystery of God's will—you, just like Peter, will need to step out of
the boat.

The Great Unknown

There have been many times in my life when, in a quest to move forward, I've had to step out of my comfort zone. I've had to stretch, trust,
and take steps forward into unknown territory.

Hillsong Church was birthed with absolutely no guarantees. There
was no promised financial support, no guarantees that people would
come, and no certainty—beyond faith in Jesus and confidence in His
calling—that God would bless this brand-new little outreach church. A
priority of safety would have kept us where we were. The church my

parents pastored was strong and flourishing, and there was a sense of inevitability that if we continued to serve their vision and live in that opportunity, the day would come when I would naturally become the senior pastor. It was clearly the safe option. But God was leading me to believe there was something more.

When I announced we were leaving and moving to the rural fringe of the city, my father never resisted it, but he was clearly in denial, and there was no official farewell. I was left to announce to the congregation myself, "This is our last Sunday." I had to buy my office desk so I could take it with me, and my friends began, in jest, to call me a disparaging name related to the area we were moving to. Yet we were excited. I never felt aggrieved about the start we were given, because I was more excited about the mysteries of the future than concerned about the comfort and safety we were leaving behind. We went out without much support and pioneered this brand-new church starting with a small group of people who attended Bible study in the area, and I guess that's all that was needed. Everything else was the great unknown.

Often people can read that story of walking on water in the book of Matthew and think, *Yeah, but Peter sank!* But we have to remind ourselves that at least Peter got out of the boat! The other disciples didn't even get *out* of the boat. That said, at least the disciples got *in* the boat—there were five thousand people who never left the shore! If you reflect for a moment on your attitude, are you more like the people who were comforted by the safety of the shore or like the disciples who took a little risk and got in the boat? Or are you like Peter, who not only left the shore but also got out of the boat, all because Jesus said, "Come"?

I have often referred to the will of God as a tightrope. Too many people think that means it is easy to fall in and out of the will of God, but He is way better at keeping us on course than we give Him credit for. I believe that when we are walking in step with the Holy Spirit, according to the Word and in the will of God, the Lord will continue to give us promptings and green lights as we keep putting one foot in front of the other. He is also well able to put red lights, warning signs, and detour billboards directly in front of us, signaling us to stop and reconsider our next moves. We just need to trust Him to direct our steps.

What has been your response when Christ has beckoned you? What have you done with the promptings in your heart and the giftings in your hand to follow Christ into the mystery of your God-given future?

Ephesians 1:9 tells us that Jesus has "made known to us the mystery of His will, according to His good pleasure." Have you ever thought about what pleases the heart of God? I have no doubt that in the mystery of your glorious future, you will have seasons of disappointment and heartache, hard times and missteps, but if you are following Christ and putting one foot in front of the other when He beckons, then His pleasure, His will, and His purpose for your life will come to pass.

Too often, I think, we long to know what is next. We'd like God to reveal the future to us in the smallest of detail, like "At five o'clock on Saturday night, a guy will walk by you on the street and bump into you. You won't think much of him at first, but stay with Me—he's the one!" Or "You know that job you went for last week? Don't take it. A week from now, a better one is going to be offered to you if you just wait."

But why would we need faith if that were the case? Why would we need to trust Him if we knew what was happening next? Life with Jesus includes stepping out into the great unknown and trusting, and it is my belief that God wants to equip us for that journey. Every circumstance and moment of life can be a new discovery about a facet of who He is and a revelation of what is to come.

Isaiah 46:10 assures us that the Lord knows "the end from the beginning." He is in all things and above all things, and His plans far outweigh your greatest desires. Embrace the mystery. Decide you're up for the adventure. You won't regret that you did.

The Myth of More

The great myth of more is that we ought to know more in our own strength, that somehow God should be explainable, understandable—that He should fit into our degree of understanding. Yet there is no understanding of God apart from a personal relationship with His Son. John 14:23 says, "Jesus answered and said to him, 'If anyone loves Me, he will keep My word; and My Father will love him, and We will come to him and make Our home with him.'"

It is easy, as a follower of Jesus Christ, to fall into the trap of doing more, as if Christian service is the single key to close relationship with our Creator. But our connection to God is all about Him and not about us. It is about what He has already done: it's His saving work on the cross and the reality of the empty grave that give us hope for the future.

As a person in full-time ministry for many years, I have watched and even been caught up in the myth that "more is more"—that somehow competing and striving and proving is what gets us ahead and that more people, more conferences, and more services will please God. But the key to having the "full riches of complete understanding" (Colossians 2:2, NIVII) is to be born again by the power of the Holy Spirit.

Walking every day in devotion with the Word of God and in step with the promptings of His Spirit will lead you into grace, peace, and the abundant life of more than you ever asked for, dreamed, or imagined, not to a place of burnout, a frantic pace, and relentless pursuit of more time, more things, and more rest. Knowing Jesus in a personal way will open up a world of endless discovery and opportunity but will never demand of you that which you cannot give.

No Longer a Mystery

It is not in riches or material wealth that we will find our peace and happiness. It is not in the "more" of earthly time, management, or fulfillment. It is in understanding the person of Jesus Christ and the depth of His sacrifice for us.

Paul tells us, "Without question, this is the great mystery of our faith," and then continues with what may be an early hymn of the church:

Christ was revealed in a human body
    and vindicated by the Spirit.
He was seen by angels
    and announced to the nations.
He was believed in throughout the world
    and taken to heaven in glory. (1 Timothy 3:16, NLT)

In that short paragraph, the Bible reveals the heart of the gospel—the mystery of godliness and life in Christ. The secret of our salvation was hidden but is now revealed. It is to those who believe in Christ that the mystery is made known.

We cannot of our own accord please God or have the abundant life we so desire without depending on Christ. In its fullest sense, the mystery of God is His plan of salvation through Jesus: His death and resurrection. And the "more" that our hearts long for is actually eternity with the One we were made to worship. We never would have been able to comprehend the way to eternal life without the coming of Jesus.

Paul says, "My purpose is that they may be encouraged in heart and united in love, so that they may have the full riches of complete understanding, in order that they may know the mystery of God, namely, Christ, in whom are hidden all the treasures of wisdom and knowledge" (Colossians 2:2–3, NIV84). In your quest to discover more, start with Jesus. Leave room for the wonder, mystery, and reverence that come along with a life in Christ. Stand in awe of a God whom we cannot understand fully, stand in wonder at the mysteries that are around every corner of His perfect will, and in your pursuit of the Ephesians 3 life, never search for more for yourself without first discovering more of Him.

3

Obedience and Abundance

I was far from a perfect kid. Growing up in the 1960s in Wellington, New Zealand, I struggled with a disproportionate need for acceptance and an overarching fear of rejection by my peers. On top of this, I faced the constant temptation that is part and parcel of adolescence and the teenage years: temptation to compromise, fit in, and seek approval.

Yet at the same time, I grew up with a strong desire to serve and honor God with my life and a belief that if I could keep myself pure in three specific areas, I would experience His abundant blessings. I believe that it was the Holy Spirit who gave me strong convictions relating to my habits, morality, and priorities. Even though youthful temptation took me to the very edges, I managed to get through my childhood and youth with those three areas of obedience intact.

Now, I know that God's grace and favor are not based on human effort and that there is nothing you can do that will make Him love you more and nothing you can do that will make Him love you less. You can't force God's hand of blessing by striving and works; it's not "Do good, get good." In fact, the Bible tells us that we have *all* sinned and fallen short of the glory of God. But I'm also certain that He honors obedience and that it can be seen and outworked through simple faithfulness. In other words, obedience and faithfulness are inseparable partners, flowing beautifully together.

Just as we can be confident that love is a doorway to marriage, discipline is necessary for weight loss, and sowing will always usher in reaping, so it is my belief that you will not experience the abundant life God promises without good old-fashioned obedience—obedience to His Word and obedience to follow His precepts and trust in His promises. Obedience is a precursor to abundance. And the best part is, if you've struggled with obedience and faithfulness in the past, there is no time like the present to begin again.

First Things First

No doubt Jesus came to earth to be an answer to human depravity—to redeem us and wear the stripes of our sin and sickness through the affliction and wounds He suffered. He also came to bring you and me resurrection life. So it's powerfully comforting that He summarizes it all with a simple contrasting statement in John 10:10: "The thief does not come except to steal, and to kill, and to destroy. I have come that they may have life, and that they may have it *more abundantly*."

Wow!

Let me explain.

Some quickly assign any thought of abundance to the afterlife and the eternal promise of fellowship with God in heaven. But take a moment to ponder the words of Jesus to His disciples after a rich young ruler had walked away in despair, unwilling to give up everything he had to take up his cross and follow Christ. This encounter left the disciples filled with questions about what hope for salvation there is for any of us, and it was in that moment that Peter took it upon himself to remind the Son of God that they had left everything to follow Him. Jesus's response to their questions was to speak specifically about the blessing that comes with putting Him first:

> Jesus answered and said, "Assuredly, I say to you, there is no one who has left house or brothers or sisters or father or mother or wife or children or lands, for My sake and the gospel's, who shall not receive a hundredfold now in this time—houses and brothers and sisters and mothers and children and lands, with persecutions—and in the age to come, eternal life. But many who are first will be last, and the last first." (Mark 10:29–31)

Notice He refers to both "now in this time" and "in the age to come" and makes a clear distinction between the two. But along with promised blessing ("now in this time"), His words are a sober reminder that persecutions are also a part of this life. Not everyone understands the blessings of God and His promises for those who live in faithful obedience.

So, what is abundance? Is it financial blessing? It could be. It's true that God can bless your business and bring abundant resources your way. His Word is clear that He blesses those who are committed to blessing others. But that's not the only thing or even the first thing that comes to mind when I think about God's overflow. To me, abundance encapsulates so much more.

The dictionary defines *abundance* as "plentifulness of the good things of life."* Think about that. Plenty of love, plenty of kindness, plenty of joy, plenty of peace, plenty of success, plenty of relationships, plenty of laughter, plenty of dessert . . . Okay, maybe that last one is just me. But "the good things of life" leaves room for a lot of interpretation!

It brings me back to the promise that motivated me to put pen to paper and write *There Is More* in the first place: "Now to Him who is able to do exceedingly abundantly above all that we ask or think, according to the power that works in us . . ." (Ephesians 3:20).

- *Exceeding:* surpassing and going beyond
- *Abundant:* full and overflowing
- *Above:* lifting you higher than you could ever ask or think

All made possible by His power working in you.

Did you know that abundance and success were among the first covenant commandments that God spoke to humans? He said to "be fruitful, multiply, replenish, and have dominion" (see Genesis 1:28). God was speaking not only about offspring but of an entire life and environment of perpetual and generational blessing and increase. This blessing and increase had a purpose then that still continues today. As I've mentioned already in this chapter, we are blessed in order to be a blessing to others and to display God's goodness in our lives. If we are to be a blessing to others, our thinking must come into agreement with what the Bible teaches about living blessed.

The key to aligning your attitude with blessing is what you put *first*

---

* *Oxford Living Dictionaries,* s.v. "abundance," https://en.oxforddictionaries.com/definition /abundance.

in your life: seek *first* His kingdom, and all these things will be added to you (see Matthew 6:33). I love that promise! But what exactly does it mean to seek first the kingdom?

Ruled by Rules

Obedience is not the most popular word these days. There are some who are telling everyone, "Be an individual—submit to no one!" Entire movements have been founded on the principles of *dis*obedience, bucking the system, steering away from the norm. Yet John 14:15 spells it out clearly when God says, "If you love Me, you will keep My commands" (HCSB).

Notice it doesn't say, "If you love Me, you will read your Bible for one hour every day, pray without ceasing, be nice to everyone, give a 10 percent tithe and 5 percent to missions, and volunteer in church." So many people allow religious practices and man-made interpretations of the Scriptures to rule their spirit. Well-meaning Christians steer people down the wrong path of regulation and ritual instead of one of living in the grace of relationship with Christ.

If you've ever been to Hillsong Church, you know that we place great value on biblical principles such as servanthood, tithing, giving, sharing the faith, and worship. But we're not bound by them! It's not an environment where you'll be kicked out if you didn't say your prayers or forgot to bring your Bible. When you walk in a true, living, dynamic relationship with Jesus Christ, obedience becomes not a sacrifice but an overflow of your love for God. Your ability to hear God's voice (and not only hear Him but listen and trust His best intentions and promises for your life) becomes the greatest driving force of your desire to obey. Seeking first the kingdom becomes a natural response rather than a forced reaction.

The Cost of More

One of the foremost examples of obedience in the Bible comes early in God's Word. The Genesis story of Abraham and Sarah bearing a promised son in their old age is one of those shout-from-the-rooftop, our-God-answers-prayer testimonies. For years, this barren woman carried the shame of her condition, while her husband waited on the fulfillment of a prophecy that he would father multitudes. *Multitudes?* From a ninety-year-old *barren* woman? Yet our God once again did the impossible. They named him Isaac, and I imagine he was the joy of their lives. He was the culmination of hope and trust, a promise and a dream that their descendants—through this small child—would be as numerous as all the stars in the sky.

So that is why I find the story of Abraham and his miracle son on a mountain in Moriah perhaps the most confronting story in the Old Testament. As a dad, my natural inclination is always to protect my children and do anything I can to keep them from harm. When they were young, it was "Please hold my hand" when crossing the road or always being careful to double-check the latch on the pool fence. As they got older, it became "Drive carefully" and "Don't be late," said kindly but firmly as they walked out the door. It would be true to say that our children tend to keep our prayer lives active, and although I have always been devoted to keeping my word and not canceling preaching appointments, if someone in my family were genuinely in pain or trouble, everything in me would want to rush to his or her side. My commitment and loyalty will always be to family.

That's why, as a dad, I can't even contemplate how it must have felt when God asked of Abraham the unthinkable:

It came to pass after these things that God tested Abraham, and said to him, "Abraham!"

And he said, "Here I am."

Then He said, "Take now your son, your only son Isaac, whom you love, and go to the land of Moriah, and offer him there as a burnt offering on one of the mountains of which I shall tell you."

So Abraham rose early in the morning and saddled his donkey, and took two of his young men with him, and Isaac his son; and he split the wood for the burnt offering, and arose and went to the place of which God had told him. Then on the third day Abraham lifted his eyes and saw the place afar off. And Abraham said to his young men, "Stay here with the donkey; the lad and I will go yonder and worship, and we will come back to you."

So Abraham took the wood of the burnt offering and laid it on Isaac his son; and he took the fire in his hand, and a knife, and the two of them went together. But Isaac spoke to Abraham his father and said, "My father!"

And he said, "Here I am, my son."

Then he said, "Look, the fire and the wood, but where is the lamb for a burnt offering?"

And Abraham said, "My son, God will provide for Himself the lamb for a burnt offering." So the two of them went together." (Genesis 22:1–8)

I've read this passage numerous times in my Christian journey. We know what comes next, but do we ever stop to think about those moments between the sacrifice and the provision? Obedience. Abraham certainly wasn't doing it because he wanted to. I imagine he was walking up that mountain trembling, wiping tears from his eyes and sweat from his brow, praying that this wasn't the moment when God would snuff out His promise.

Think of the conversation when Isaac looked at his father, confusion and innocence on his face. "But Daddy, where is the sheep to kill?"

Abraham's response—"God Himself will provide the lamb"—was faith filled, but his actions were defining. He didn't just stop at lip service. The Scriptures tell us he bound his son, laid sticks around him, placed him on the altar, and raised his hand to slay his boy.

Obedience is costly.

Trust the Provider

In Abraham's hand he held his boy, in his heart he held his promise, and in his obedience the Lord provided.

> The Angel of the LORD called to him from heaven and said, "Abraham, Abraham!"
>
> So he said, "Here I am."
>
> And He said, "Do not lay your hand on the lad, or do anything to him; for now I know that you fear God, since you have not withheld your son, your only son, from Me."
>
> Then Abraham lifted his eyes and looked, and there behind him was a ram caught in a thicket by its horns. So Abraham went and took the ram, and offered it up for a burnt offering instead of his son. And Abraham called the name of the place, The-LORD-Will-Provide; as it is said to this day, "In the Mount of the LORD it shall be provided."

Then the Angel of the LORD called to Abraham a second time out of heaven, and said: "By Myself I have sworn, says the LORD, because you have done this thing, and have not withheld your son, your only son—blessing I will bless you, and multiplying I will multiply your descendants as the stars of the heaven and as the sand which is on the seashore; and your descendants shall possess the gate of their enemies. In your seed all the nations of the earth shall be blessed, because you have obeyed My voice." (verses 11–18)

Can you digest those promises? *Blessings:* "I will bless you." *Fruitfulness:* "I will multiply you." And the blessing didn't stop with Abraham, for God said that because of his obedience, the nations would also be blessed.

I want to suggest to you that there is "more" on the other side of your obedience, both now and in the future. Your ability to hold fast to the promises of God, trust in His provision, and believe that His desire for your life is abundance will hold you in good stead time and time again. That when the difficult times, the testing times, the waiting times, and the trying times come, Jehovah-Jireh, the Lord our Provider, is walking ten steps ahead, purposing the above-all-you-could-ask-or-imagine life, both here and in eternity.

Abraham's initial promise (found in Genesis 15) was for numerous descendants. His reward for obedience was an honor bestowed on him that would outlast time. You see, Abraham was to become the patriarch of the Davidic line that would lead to Christ. It was obedience that led him to abundantly above all he could ask or imagine.

What a promise! What a hope we have! Unlike Abraham, we have been given all the promises of abundant life and all the parameters of holy living—without the sacrifice. As 1 Samuel 15:22 says, "Obedience is better than sacrifice" (NLT).

Upward Falling

On Hillsong UNITED'S *Empires* album, there is a song—"Touch the Sky"—that is a favorite of mine and is an anthem that has come to mean a lot to our church. Its lyrics admonish us that life with Christ is often found in a posture of surrender and that obedience to His call leads to abundance for us.

> My heart beating, my soul breathing
> I found my life when I laid it down
> Upward falling, spirit soaring
> I touch the sky when my knees hit the ground.†

As I sing these words, I am reminded again of the God dream that Abraham was given about the innumerable stars in the sky. This dream of the stars was carved out in Abraham's obedience, walked out in the dust of the desert sands.

The apostle John wrote, "Anyone who claims to be intimate with God ought to live the same kind of life Jesus lived" (1 John 2:6, MSG). What a challenge! If the life we want is a full one—filled to overflowing with exceeded dreams and fulfilled promises—we must find ourselves

---

† Words and music by Joel Houston, Dylan Thomas, and Michael Guy Chislett, "Touch the Sky," *Empires*, copyright © 2015 Hillsong Music Publishing. Used by permission.

before the King, surrendered and obedient. We must be willing to hit the ground before we touch the sky.

Costly Compromise

Just as the mystery of more has everything to do with knowing Jesus, so the journey of more must ultimately be about obeying Him. But our obedience must not fall victim to pragmatism or convenience and must never be in disagreement with the conviction of the Holy Spirit.

King Saul's whole reign was brought to an end because although he sacrificed the burnt offerings as a ritual, he did it in an environment of excuses, interpretation, and ultimately disobedience (see 1 Samuel 13:1–14).

Saul was in the eye of the storm in Gilgal. Samuel the prophet had departed after telling Saul he would return in a week and leaving the king with explicit instructions that no sacrifice be made until he— Samuel, acting as God's mouthpiece—returned. But the tense environment meant that pressure was mounting on Saul. Thousands of Philistine men, horses, and chariots were surging toward them. The Israelites were completely outnumbered and trembling with fear. The Bible narrative paints a picture of Saul's men in jeopardy and with distress levels at an all-time high as they ran for the hills in the most literal sense. We are told that many hid in caves, thickets, rocks, holes, and pits, while others escaped altogether, crossing the Jordan in their panicked efforts to get away.

Saul could see that his men were quickly descending into a rabble, and after waiting for Samuel for seven days, he took matters into his own hands. He made the sacrifices and burnt offerings he was so clearly told not to make until the priest returned.

When Samuel returned, Saul offered every conceivable excuse he could muster, but Samuel had only bad news for the king. It wasn't God's plan for Saul to interpret the Word of the Lord, adjusting commandments to fit the circumstances. It was clear to everyone that Saul was a leader with more faith in his own judgment than in God, who had anointed him Israel's first king. His disobedience cost him his kingdom.

How often in our journey through life do our pressing circumstances seem to give us every logical reason to translate, decipher, and interpret the Word of God in a manner that suits us rather than to simply trust and obey? No matter how compelling the inner voice of pragmatism sounds, when God's Word says, "Let your 'Yes' be 'Yes' and your 'No' be 'No'" (Matthew 5:37, WEB), it doesn't mean that we can simply understand it as yes until it doesn't suit us and then interpret things as no until it's inconvenient. Compromising on our beliefs or misinterpreting the truth of God's Word will never attract abundance and blessing.

As a pastor of a church, I am regularly asked by the media about my thoughts on current affairs and prominent social issues. I constantly feel as if the premise behind the questions is flawed. I don't believe that "What do you think?" is the right question to ask, as what I think can so quickly descend into pragmatism, clichés, and compromise. I could so easily respond by saying such things as "Everyone deserves to be happy" and "It's not my job to judge others" or even "Live and let live." And that might be what I think. But is that what *really* matters?

Obedience to God and His Word is the only right way for me to responsibly shepherd His people. And it's ultimately my commitment to obey God that will keep His abundance and blessing flowing in my life and ministry and in the church that I've been honored to pastor all these years. Sometimes that means taking the hard road when it's the right road to take.

I have little regard for the harsh spirit behind those who sit on the sidelines, spitting vehement judgment and self-righteous vitriol at people who may be on the other side of the fence from where they sit. To me, it is an agonizing choice to commit to obedience to God and His Word if I feel it may hurt someone's feelings or paint me in a negative light, but I have seen the fallout that accompanies compromise. I have looked on as any trace of abundance has dried up for people who have allowed obedience to Christ and His Word to be eroded by convenient interpretation rather than faithful obedience.

The life of grace we are called to is fueled by our love of the Savior. As we turn our eyes on Jesus, study His Word, and trust in His promises, it will become easier to live in obedience, discard convenience, and simply obey rather than interpret.

Go a Little Deeper

I'll leave you with one of my favorite Bible stories. It's in Luke 5, when Jesus gives His disciples a lesson in exactly this way of thinking. Simon Peter and the others had recently hauled in their fishing gear after a disappointing night. Likely, they had just cleaned their nets—no small task—and reordered their boat, hoping that tomorrow their luck would change, when Jesus spoke to them. He said, "Put out into the deep [water], and lower your nets for a haul" (verse 4, AMPC). Who doesn't like a haul?

But Peter's response to Jesus is exactly what so many of us would say, and it's shrouded with doubts and excuses: "Master, we've worked hard all night and haven't caught anything" (verse 5, NIVII). What he was really saying was "But Jesus, I don't *feel* like doing it. I really don't *want* to do it." Despite Peter's human response, he shows his love and devotion to Christ by saying, "But because you say so, I will let down the nets" (verse 5, NIVII).

The Bible goes on to tell us, "When they had done so, they caught such a large number of fish that their nets began to break. So they signaled their partners in the other boat to come and help them, and they came and filled both boats so full that they began to sink" (verses 6–7, NIVII).

Relax—their boat didn't sink! It was simply weighed down by blessings. Their portion was the abundant, overflowing, more-than-enough blessings that only God Himself could bring.

Even in deep waters your obedience matters. Actually, *especially* in deep waters your obedience matters. It's in these moments, when we're fragile and in danger of making poor choices, that we are most susceptible to the Enemy. Even when you don't feel like it, when it doesn't make sense, when it's inconvenient and frustrating listening to Jesus, trusting His voice and obeying His commands will *always* exceed your expectations.

4

Gifted and Graced

Three hundred sextillion. Now, that's a big number! Three hundred sextillion—that's how many stars are estimated to be in our universe. Three hundred sextillion burning little lights, suspended in space and twinkling night in and night out, created by God for our viewing pleasure. Wow! And not only did God create every single star, He also named them all!

> He determines the number of the stars
> and calls them each by name. (Psalm 147:4, NIVII)

Discovering more of who Jesus is means discovering more of the Father. The Trinitarian God we serve has relationship with us through God the Father, Christ the Son, and the Holy Spirit. And the Bible gives us lots of insight into the character and nature of each of them and how they work and relate alongside us. When it comes to you and your unique gifts and the grace upon your life to outwork the plans and purposes He has for you, *nothing* gets past the Father.

Good Good Father

Have you ever opened a present, only to discover something that either (a) you had no idea what it was or (b) you really didn't want what was inside the box?

My wife, Bobbie, is a brilliant gift giver. She is extravagantly generous and spends huge amounts of time and energy pondering the person for whom she is buying a gift and picking out the perfect present. She does this not only for our family but also for our friends, our team, and many other significant people in our lives.

As for me, I may not have always gotten it right.

When I was eleven or twelve, my mother gave each of my four siblings and me a little money to buy Christmas presents. With excitement in our eyes and a bounce in our step, we caught the train into the city of Wellington and began our search for the perfect gifts. My search landed me in Woolworths (similar to a Target store), which is where I spotted "it." My eye was caught by what I thought was a dazzling piece of jewelry, just perfect for my older sister, Maureen. And it was cheap, so it fit nicely within my meager budget. I was so excited about this gift that I took it home and immediately wrapped it and placed it under the Christmas tree in the living room.

I will never forget the look on Maureen's face as she opened it on Christmas day. "What is it?" she asked with a confused and disappointed tone. This thoughtful gift of priceless jewelry turned out to be a cheap silver-plated key ring, which was of very little use to my sister, who was not yet old enough to own a car or have need of a key ring.

The good news for you is that God is not short of ideas when it comes to the gifts He brings into your life. And the Bible tells us that every one of those gifts is good. As James 1:17 says, "Every good thing given and every perfect gift is from above, coming down from the Father of lights, with whom there is no variation or shifting shadow" (NASB). In other words, there are no cheap silver-plated key rings coming from God.

Our God is the God of more. Yes, when it comes to lavishing gifts upon humanity, the God of three hundred sextillion stars has never been short of ideas, and His purpose for you is good, perfect, and filled with abundant life. First Peter 4:10 speaks of the "manifold grace of God" (NASB) that bestows gifts on His children. *Manifold* literally means "many folds" or "many shades and colors," so we're talking about a kaleidoscope of multicolored, multifaceted gifts! And each and every one of them is aligned with God's will and specifically assigned for His purpose.

When you think of your life, what are the gifts that come to mind? Do you even believe that you are gifted? Gifted with heaven-sent, perfectly curated, irreplaceable, and unique gifts? Let me assure you that you are.

Perhaps there are some that seem like obvious gifts: ministry and spiritual gifts such as apostleship, evangelism, healing, and prophecy (see Ephesians 4:7–16; Romans 12:3–8). God-breathed natural gifts such as singing, dancing, writing, and communication gifts can also be easy to pinpoint. But beyond some of these more obvious ones, life itself is a gift, breath is a gift, friends are gifts, family is a gift. Do you see the people in your life as gifts? And did you know that God has put people and talents in your life that are directly related to the plans and purposes He has for you? Perhaps you don't feel as though you can identify your own giftings. Maybe you're holding back when it comes to some of the talents within you simply because you are afraid of what the future will look like. Or maybe someone has spoken poorly of you or downplayed the gifts in your hand.

As a pastor, I see it as a huge responsibility and honor to steward the gifts within people's lives. So allow me to pastor you for a moment . . .

You *are* gifted.

You *are* talented.

Your gifts are *good* and *perfect* and come from the same God who knows the stars and calls them by name.

And your gifts and talents are perfectly poised to enable you to fulfill the plans and purposes of God for your life.

Unwavering Belief

Unbelief, disbelief, and misbelief—each one is different. What do you believe about the plans and purposes that God has for your life? I would dare say that each and every one of us has questioned whether God really does have good plans and good purposes for us.

The definition of unbelief is "an absence of faith." Plain and simple, it is the lack of belief in something or someone.

My prayer is that you are not struggling with unbelief—that, yes, your faith may waver at moments, but you ultimately are not absent of belief when it comes to knowledge that the God of the universe loves, values, cares for, and wants the best for you. I pray that even in difficult times, you will choose belief over unbelief and that your faith in the Father of lights will be unwavering, steady, and trustworthy, just as His love for you is as well.

The gospel of Mark records the story of a man bringing his son to Jesus during one of His public meetings near the Mount of Transfiguration. People were pushing and shoving and trying to speak to Jesus. They were discussing His ministry when the man came forward, saying, "Teacher, I brought You my son, who has a mute spirit. And wherever it seizes him, it throws him down; he foams at the mouth, gnashes his teeth, and becomes rigid. So I spoke to Your disciples, that they should cast it out, but they could not" (9:17–18).

Here's the exchange that happened next:

[Jesus asked the father], "How long has this been happening to him?"

And he said, "From childhood. And often he has thrown him both into the fire and into the water to destroy him. But if You can do anything, have compassion on us and help us."

Jesus said to him, "If you can believe, all things are possible to him who believes."

Immediately the father of the child cried out and said with tears, "Lord, I believe; help my unbelief!" (verses 21–24)

Did you know that this man was not suffering from unbelief as we commonly understand it? He wasn't completely lacking all faith, but he was certainly suffering from disbelief. Disbelief is *wanting* to believe something but having a hard time doing so. It's perhaps better described as doubt. We've all struggled with disbelief at least a time or two.

In early 1991, I was strolling along downtown Sydney's major thoroughfare, George Street, browsing the shops and enjoying a rest day with our South African guest, who was in town to minister to our thriving, but not overly large, congregation. In a moment of conversational silence, he suddenly stopped, swung around, and said to me, "Brian, you will have a church of ten thousand people in this city one day—you just wait and see." And then he carried on walking.

I hesitated at his words. Everything in me wanted to believe that what he said was true, but I couldn't get my head around it. Ten thousand? Where would they come from? This is Australia—people don't flock to church here. Where would we put them all? (Practical problems first.) I've always been a dreamer, so I knew that his prophetic words over me weren't entirely crazy. What I had wasn't unbelief; it was disbelief.

Disbelief can stunt us and keep us from living fully. It can limit the potential within us by quenching the things that God has set apart for our future. It can hold us back from the more that God intends for our lives.

David Brooks, an American journalist and political commentator, once said, "Most successful people begin with two beliefs: the future can be better than the present, and I have the power to make it so."* Well, time has proved that ten thousand was a complete underestimation. Twenty-five years on, by the grace of God, we are exceeding that almost four times over!

I have three children who are all artistic, each with a natural eye for creativity, design, and graphic arts. They have a talent clearly inherited from their mum, because unlike the rest of my family, I have next to no skill with a pencil or paintbrush in my hand. I admire such gifts in other people, but for years I underestimated the value of the gifts God had given to me.

---

* David Brooks, "Lost in the Crowd," *New York Times,* December 15, 2008, www.nytimes.com /2008/12/16/opinion/16brooks.html.

It took me a long time to realize that my leadership gift is not something everyone has. I was functioning in my gifting and being successful, but because it came so naturally to me, it felt normal. I am continuously looking for solutions and often trying to find a way forward, so when churches that I was planting were flourishing, I didn't realize this was my gift! But in reality, I was gifted in leadership, and it was then that I learned that not everyone could see the things I saw and that although some decisions were obvious to me, they were not always obvious to everyone else. *Anyone can do that,* I used to think. But I learned that when it came to intuitive leadership, not everyone can.

It is human nature to underestimate our own gifting while overestimating the need for us to possess the skills we lack and that someone else might have.

I was in my twenties when I recognized my leadership gifting and committed to maximizing it, and I began planting churches then that not only still exist today but are strong, established churches influencing a lot of people. I was walking in both my gifting and God's grace.

What you believe about who God is and what He has set apart for your future makes all the difference in achieving the "abundantly above" life you desire. God doesn't gift you one way to use you another. God isn't double minded! So, can I encourage you? Carefully measure your disbelief and continually confess the promises of God over your life. Don't simply believe in the power of your dreams; speak life and courage into the possibilities before you.

Now, *mis*belief is a whole other ball game. Misbelief is believing something that is simply untrue. When it comes to James 1:17 and to God and gifts, there are *many* misbeliefs out there.

Not Good? Not a Gift!

There are many things I do not know, but here is something I do: temptation, sickness, disease, and poverty are *not* gifts from God. For too long, too many people have tried to pin some of these devastating circumstances on God. But let us never become deceived about what comes from Him and what doesn't.

The world is filled with broken things. Horrible things. Hurtful things. Over and over we can be disappointed by the hypocrisy inside our own homes or inside our hearts. We can wrongly judge and come to false conclusions. We can kneel at our bedsides, hearts poured out to God, and still, like doubting Thomas (see John 20:24–29), demand proof that God didn't cause that bad thing to happen.

But take it from me, my friend, what makes a gift good is that the very nature and character of God is good. Furthermore, the apostle James tells us that He is unchanging. If you're stuck in a place where you feel as if nothing is good, then be reminded that there are no shifting shadows within God. His plans and purposes and abundant promises in your life—His gifts—are *always* good.

Everyone Makes Mistakes

The Word of our unchanging Lord says, "By Him all things were created that are in heaven and that are on earth, visible and invisible, whether thrones or dominions or principalities or powers. All things were created through Him and for Him" (Colossians 1:16).

You were created by God and for God. When He places gifts in your life, He gives you the grace to steward them well. And when you do, He gets the glory! But there are three main mistakes people make with their gifts.

The truth is, gifts are attractive. Whether we wrap them up with perfectly matching paper and bows or simply present them with a smile, gifts are meant to be appealing. It's no surprise, then, that the good and perfect gifts in your life will also appear attractive. So the first mistake is putting our attention on the gift rather than on the Gift Giver. In other words, it's easy to make our gifts all about us. Instead, always remember who and what your gifts are for.

We were created to worship God—created to be in intimate relationship with Him and show His manifest glory working in and through our lives. Don't ever be overly enamored with people's praise. Resist the temptation to feel more important than you are or put too much emphasis on your skill or talent, but instead recognize where it came from and why God gave it to you in the first place.

And in the same way, don't ever be too swayed by criticism. I have personally experienced some pretty hurtful criticism in my life—some totally unfounded, some that turned out to be a valuable lesson, and some that said more about the critic than it said about me. While we are constantly learning along the journey of life, we cannot allow critics to shape our beliefs in what we know to be true and what we have heard from God. Be steadfast and unmoving in your convictions when it comes to the gifts and talents that God has put in your life and the purposes for which He has called you.

Another common mistake people make with their giftings is comparing them with those of others. Comparison is the thief of joy. Don't do it! What God has placed in your life is unique and special, and what He has placed in the lives of others is unique and special. Each comes with its own set of blessings and challenges, many that you would never know unless you walked a mile in someone else's shoes. It is a lie to think that God would ever run out of gifts or that just because He has given someone else a measure of the gifting you desire, He can't do the same for you. Remember, three hundred sextillion stars! Our God is endlessly creative and boundless in generosity. He is never empty handed.

The last mistake is letting your gifts determine your value. What you do is not who you are. Your value is in who you are and whose you are. Gifts are not bestowed upon you because you earned them—those are rewards. Gifts are bestowed upon you because you are a loved, valued, and chosen son or daughter of the Most High God.

Don't Be the Last to See

What is it about us men? It feels as though I have embarrassed myself three hundred sextillion times by adamantly telling Bobbie that something is not where she said it was in the pantry or fridge. After insisting a number of times that it is indeed there, Bobbie will eventually come and pick it up from the exact spot I have been hopelessly staring at!

Gifts can be just like that. Sometimes the slowest person to see your gift is yourself. Being blinded by insecurity or perhaps being disappointed by the past or fearing the future can blur your vision. But don't underestimate how well God has set you up to live the life you're called to live.

Imagine if someone you loved spent weeks scoping out the perfect present just for you. She sought out your favorite things, put effort into the search, spent time and money on the gift, and went to great lengths to make you happy, only to have you ignore the present, refuse to look at it, decline to open it, or see no real value in it.

Well, the God of the sun, moon, and stars wants to give you good and perfect gifts. Not only does He know exactly what you need, but at the same time He's bringing your gifts to maturity, He is opening doors of opportunity that perfectly match those gifts. Receive them. Don't downplay, hide, or misuse the gifts that are upon your life; they serve a purpose not only here on earth but for eternity as well.

Almost forty years ago, our firstborn son, Joel Timothy Houston, arrived into our world, and we were never the same. As the nurse took this little red bundle and placed him on those cold scales, a gasp of disbelief was audible from her colleagues. They declared him to be more than ten pounds in weight and explained that he was a remarkable twenty-four inches tall! Sure, these attributes of his were measurable, but what we didn't know in that hospital room were the immeasurable gifts, talents, and potential that only his heavenly Father could see. When he was a newborn, the gifts and talents were clearly latent and the potential within him unseen by all in the room. The gifts added nothing to his physical weight, but their weightiness and value now consistently bear witness to millions around the world. And as his father, I believe that the best is still yet to come.

We all have within us gifts that may still be latent, unrecognizable by both ourselves and others, but they are there. How do these gifts emerge? The starting point is simply believing that you are indeed gifted with unique talents that are thoughtfully wired into your DNA from the moment you were conceived in the mind of God. And it is these gifts that are instruments perfectly handcrafted for the more that God has in store for you.

You don't have to be smart. You don't have to be pretty. You don't have to have all the answers or be able to do all the talking. You don't have to be articulate, and your circumstances don't have to be perfect. You simply have to believe. There is always more potential, more progress, and more purpose to be found when you believe that you are not only gifted but also graced.

And don't forget to look up. Hesitate before you close the curtains, and stare heavenward at the Creator's masterpiece. He loves you more than you could ever imagine. I pray that every time you gaze into the night sky, you will remember that God's gifts are limitless and that His thoughts for you outnumber the stars.

5

Calling and
Confession

Lemony Snicket, the pen name of American novelist Daniel Handler, sure had a way of painting a despairing picture of what life looks like when we are resigned to fate. He said, "Fate is like a strange, unpopular restaurant, filled with odd little waiters who bring you things you never asked for and don't always like."*

According to the it-has-to-be-this-way belief, life is simply a series of events that happen *to* us. There is no way around it: if we live long enough, we will all experience grief and disappointment, heartache and pain. But unlike Lemony Snicket's picture, the one you paint of your life and the words that you speak over your future, in spite of the mountains you will climb, doesn't have to look like the inside of a dirty diner or an unfriendly local eatery, where you groan with resignation, presuming that the service will be slow and the food ordinary.

Fate is a world of endless futility. It gives up before you start and sees

---

* Lemony Snicket and Brett Helquist, *The Slippery Slope,* A Series of Unfortunate Events, Book 10 (New York: HarperCollins, 2003), 21.

no world beyond the inevitable and no expectation of hope beyond the feasible. Fate accepts a negative report without a fight and waves the white flag of surrender at the first sign of an obstacle. And fate speaks defeat without any regard for the negativity that it brings to your soul and the hearts of those around you. "It was meant to be" becomes a lyric spoken all too quickly. But is there a better way?

Oh yes, there is! Instead, we can live secure in our calling, confident in the God who called us, and wide awake with hope for the future if we just hold fast to our confession of faith.

The Power of the Tongue

Have you ever held within your power the ability to make a difference between life and death? The answer is yes. Proverbs 18:21 tells us clearly, "Death and life are in the power of the tongue."

As with the Lemony Snicket quote, words can paint a picture—perhaps one of despair or one of hope. They can bring life and solution to a situation, or they can bring fear and pain.

Young children have had their entire worldview framed through the harsh words of a neglectful parent or their beliefs shaped by the careless words of a frustrated teacher. Marriages have ended over the sharp words of a wounded spouse with an untamed tongue.

The Bible exhorts us over and over to be careful with our words. For instance:

Kind words heal and help;
    cutting words wound and maim. (Proverbs 15:4, MSG)

I tell you that men will have to give account on the day of judgment for every careless word they have spoken. For by your words you will be acquitted, and by your words you will be condemned. (Matthew 12:36–37, NIV84)

What do your words say about you? And does your confession (the things that come out of your mouth, the meditations of your heart, and the thoughts that regularly play over and over in your mind) line up with your calling? Just as God doesn't *gift* us and then fail to *grace* us, He doesn't *call* us without first *equipping* us.

Faith Has a Sound

Have you ever wondered what faith sounds like? The Bible tells us you can *hear* faith. Galatians 3:5 says, "He who supplies the Spirit to you and works miracles among you, does He do it by the works of the law, or by the hearing of faith?"

God hears what we are believing for. Maybe you're longing for something new: a fresh start or an answer to prayer. Perhaps you're desperate for healing or hoping that a loved one will find peace. Maybe you are believing that God will provide for you in this next season. Faith needs to be spoken. It needs to be heard, because when it is heard, it has power.

Many years ago, before we had any buildings to house our congregation, we had to move from a warehouse we were renting because we knew it was too small for our growing church. It was during this time that a teenager from our youth ministry started to talk to me about the old city-council buildings that had recently been shut down. They had been sold to a huge multinational company planning to build a mall, but work and permits had yet to be organized. This young guy had a vision in his heart and an enthusiastic mix of both faith and energy, and even though he was confronted by my skepticism, he took it upon himself to reach out to this large organization and share with them about our growing church and all the great things we were doing locally within our community. You wouldn't believe it, but that large multinational organization agreed to give our church a lease on the old council buildings (perfect for our midweek hub and big enough to house our college, youth ministry, and offices) with a month-to-month contract for a dollar a year! I have often joked that Bobbie and I prayed about it and decided to pay that rent all by ourselves.

At first the owners said they would simply lease it to us for a short time, maybe three to six months. However, that building served us for almost *seven* years—enough time for us to raise a deposit and buy our first piece of land in a prime location. And wait for the punch line: when we finally received notice that we would need to vacate so the building could be demolished (six and a half fruitful years later), it was exactly the same week we received the keys for our own church home. It was a miracle! And it all stemmed from the confession of a young man not yet twenty years of age and his willingness to speak his faith out loud.

Faith is a different language. It sees through obstacles and over mountains. It believes the best and hopes unswervingly. What do people hear when you open your mouth? Are they hearing faith? Are they able to see what you're believing for?

A Holy Representative

Jesus is called the "High Priest of our confession" in Hebrews 3:1. Let me explain that image. In the Old Testament era, the high priest stood between the people and God. He would bring sacrifices on behalf of the people in order for them to be made acceptable to God. Now, under the New Covenant, Jesus Himself is our representative, making our case to God the Father through His constant intercession. Unlike in the old era, we no longer need to bring sacrifices every day to be made whole; instead, Jesus Himself was offered as the perfect and blameless sacrifice.

So, if Christ is our representative and is represented by what we say, then we ought to be careful about what we say! Does your confession line up with the Word of God?

Our confession is meant to be an affirmation of truth and a declaration of God's Word and His will. Our human nature is ruled by what we see, and I think that if we are being honest with ourselves, what we see is not always worthy of our confession. Despite our feelings and despite our circumstances, however, we must always align ourselves with God's Word and declare it to be true.

This doesn't mean denying reality or making false claims. Instead, it is about standing in faith, recognizing that our circumstances may be temporary but that our unchanging God has made us eternal promises.

Hebrews 13:15 in The Message says this: "Let's take our place outside with Jesus, no longer pouring out the sacrificial blood of animals but pouring out sacrificial praises from our lips to God in Jesus' name." The Old Testament sacrifice was a lamb without blemish; the New Testament sacrifice is words without blemish. Confessing the name of Jesus

Christ as Lord is the only sacrifice required to enter the kingdom of God.

Let that sink in as you think about the words you speak to your friends and your enemies, your colleagues and your children, your future and your calling. Don't allow condemnation to rob you when it comes to your confession. God is not only the high priest of our confession but also our gracious Father, our precious Savior, and our merciful God. Stand on the promises He has made and have faith that the Son of Man is forever interceding on your behalf.

Speak Your Faith

I will never forget the sad and embarrassed countenances of a small group of my fellow students at Christian Life Bible College in Wellington, New Zealand, in the early 1970s. They stared from the porch of our college accommodation down the driveway and toward the road, wondering why they couldn't see the new car that was supposed to arrive that very day to transport them the four hundred miles from Wellington to Auckland for a weekend ministry trip. You see, one of the students had been saying for weeks that on a certain date and at a certain time, God would provide—by faith—a brand-new car. Well, this was that day, and there was no car to be seen. Needless to say, the trip never occurred. Was it faith or presumption?

A similar scenario was told to me by an airline employee who worked behind the check-in counter at Sydney's bustling Kingsford Smith Airport. Having recognized me as the Hillsong pastor, she launched into a story of a recent group of students from another church and denomination who'd arrived at the airport fully packed and ready to fly off on a short-term mission trip. On request, however, they were unable to produce tickets for their destination. They confidently declared they had tickets "by faith." But did they fly that day? Unfortunately not. And what's more, they were dismissed as a nuisance on what was just another busy morning for the airline staff.

Sadly, the wonderful truth of speaking "words of life" over a situation has been misused over the years by some who have mixed presumption and greed into biblical truth. They have stirred together a dangerous concoction of imbalance and deception, which in turn has given birth to an equally dangerous, but polar opposite, reaction by those who reject the notion of faith. This gives those people room to write off the "silliness" of faith as "blab and grab" or "name it and claim it." I'm sure that this kind of imbalance and the perversion of truth is one of the devil's favorite strategies for locking people out of powerful truth, but it's a simple case of throwing out the baby with the bathwater.

What separates a faith confession from empty words of presumption? The difference is a fine line. It has a lot to do with our motives, alignment with the Word of God, and good old-fashioned godly wisdom (see Proverbs 24:3).

In the early years of Hillsong Church, one of our key volunteers called me to ask for prayer, as he'd had an accident at work and damaged the retina in his eye, which caused him severe pain. I told him to come on in, and along with another one of our pastors, I laid hands on him, believed for his healing, and prayed.

As we spoke our prayers out loud, he began to shout, "I'm healed!"

With shock in my voice and my inner doubting Thomas rising from within me, I asked him, "Are you sure?"

To my dismay, he started to remove the bandage the doctor had just positioned over his eye to keep the light out. As it turns out, his confession of healing was absolutely real, a genuine miracle, but I still insisted that he return to the doctor to confirm that he no longer needed the bandages. I simply saw it as common sense, which Solomon described as "discretion" in Proverbs 2:10–11:

> When wisdom enters your heart,
> And knowledge is pleasant to your soul,
> Discretion will preserve you;
> Understanding will keep you.

Discretion will preserve you? Yes. *Discretion* can be defined as common sense, and *preserve* simply means that it will keep you on course. But genuine wisdom, discretion, and discernment do not speak words of defeat instead of words of life and do not carelessly spew out hopelessness rather than hopefulness.

The Power of Praise

Never underestimate the power of your words to bring change—to see chains broken and miracles come to life. Praise and thanksgiving to God are paramount in order to lift our eyes above the circumstances we are facing and place them firmly on the Word of faith, Jesus.

Would you change the way you lived and spoke if you knew that every word and thought would be examined by God first? David asked that God approve his words and reflections as though they were offerings brought to the altar:

Let the words of my mouth and meditation of my heart
Be acceptable in Your sight,
O LORD, my strength and my Redeemer. (Psalm 19:14)

Would you turn the worship music up louder and the reality television off more quickly?

Would you slow down in your anger toward your children or your spouse and choose your words carefully, knowing that what you say holds great weight?

Perhaps you have sickness in your body and for years have suffered with pain and turmoil. Does your confession, though not ignoring reality, point to the promises of God that one day we will all be healed and whole? Do you have faith that the same God who healed blind Bartimaeus, lying by a dirt road with little else but his faith, still wants to heal you? Mark 10 documents the account of this man who called out, even amid ridicule, believing that Jesus of Nazareth could heal him.

When Jesus took notice of him, He said, "What do you want Me to do for you?"

The blind man replied to him, "Rabboni, that I may receive my sight."

Jesus told him, "Go your way; your *faith* has made you well." Immediately he received his sight and followed Him on the way (see verses 51–52).

His *faith* made him whole. His confession and his cries attracted the heart of the Savior and drew Him close.

Did you know that Jesus still walks the dusty streets of our lives today? That He waits to be beckoned, waits for our confession of faith and proclamation of miracles so that He can move close, bend low, and bring healing, help, and solution?

There is a reason our church begins every church service with praise and thanksgiving. I once heard someone write off the faster praise songs at the beginning of a service as the cocktails served before the meal. But there is a whole lot more to the songs of praise that we commence every service with than simply giving the latecomers a chance to arrive. Praise is always an entry point and often precedes the miracle:

> Enter his gates with thanksgiving
> > and his courts with praise. (Psalm 100:4, NIV11)

Besides the tradition of worship being the right thing to do, singing and speaking the Word of God can actually bring a felt shift to the atmosphere of a church service. Worship brings a tangible sense of joy and peace, power and awe, into the room as we confess with our lips the greatness of who God is. Worship is also filling the human spirit with the content of God's Word, which is why we take such great care when approving the lyrics of our songs. We know that songs can shape theology and that theology builds faith.

Confess the name of Jesus. The Bible tells us that it is our confession in Him as the risen Lord that puts us into right standing with God and changes our position from that of outsider to that of close ally. Jesus is the beginning and the center of our faith confession and also the culmination. The Bible tells us that when we align our wills with His (practically speaking, this means aligning our wills with His Word and His promise), all that we ask, in Jesus, will be done. As Proverbs says,

Put GOD in charge of your work,

then what you've planned will take place.

(Proverbs 16:3, MSG)

If your soul is in despair or your circumstances seem impossible, then lift your hands, shout unto God, beckon His presence, sing your faith, give a sacrifice of praise, and watch as the Word of God and power of your confession change your future.

Speak It into Being

Words are not just for communication; words are for creation. Before Adam and Eve ever fell into sin, they knew God only as Elohim: the God who creates. Before they ever needed Jehovah-Jireh (Provider) or Jehovah-Rapha (Healer), they were in communion with the Creator God.

You see, the Lord created the world with His words. He said, "Let there be light" (Genesis 1:3). And there was light.

Our words *still* hold creative power. They can breathe life into dead situations, create hope where there was none. *You* can speak life into your marriage, your spouse, your partner. You can speak destiny and purpose into your children's little bodies, helping them create belief around the words you choose. You can speak life into your well-being and your finances. It's as easy as thanking God for what you do have and trusting Him with your words for what you don't. Recall scriptures that relate to your circumstances and speak them out over your life. For example, you might echo Philippians 4:19: "Thank You, God, that You supply *all* my needs in accordance to Your riches in glory!"

Perhaps it's important to explain what I'm *not* saying. I'm not talking about holding God hostage by saying "Thank You, Lord, for a million dollars" and expecting Him to add several extra zeros to your bank account balance. But you can speak the Word of God into the world around you and watch Him bring miraculous change and breakthrough to seemingly desperate situations.

Remember this: when God tells you to do something, He enables you to make it happen.

God *said,* "Let there be light" (Genesis 1:3).

Noah *preached* deliverance and received it (see Hebrews 11:7).

Moses *decreed* the plagues (see Exodus 7–11).

Elijah *spoke* drought into being (see 1 Kings 17:1).

Joshua *commanded* the sun and moon to stand still (see Joshua 10:12).

Shadrach, Meshach, and Abednego *confessed* the Word (see Daniel 3:17).

Jesus *proclaimed* His resurrection (see Matthew 16:21).

And the list goes on. What are you believing for? What is the "more" when it comes to your calling that stirs you to make a confession of faith? Speak, proclaim, command, and call down the blessing that is promised to you. Lift your eyes and lift your confession; then watch our High Priest lift your spirits and cause to rise within you hope and faith that He will do abundantly above all you could ever ask or imagine.

The Ultimate Confession of Faith

Jesus Himself knew who He was and what He was called to. He spoke out His calling as a proclamation of faith:

The Spirit of the LORD is upon Me,

Because He has anointed Me

To preach the gospel to the poor;

He has sent Me to heal the brokenhearted,

To proclaim liberty to the captives

And recovery of sight to the blind,

To set at liberty those who are oppressed;

To proclaim the acceptable year of the LORD. (Luke 4:18–19)

Jesus knew the Spirit of the Lord was upon Him, and it was upon Him to fulfill that which He was called to. It was a confession of His calling. He confessed His calling, and at the same time, His calling was for confession: "to *preach* the gospel . . . to *proclaim* liberty . . ."

What are you called to? What has the Lord placed in your spirit and your heart that is uniquely yours? Perhaps it is something you have resisted, or maybe it is something you have never even claimed. Can I encourage you? Confess your faith. Profess your calling. Stand firm on the Word of God and speak it over your life with boldness and conviction. The Spirit of the Lord is upon you, too.

With God's Word in your heart and His name on your lips, there is no obstacle, no mountain, no disappointment or resignation to fate that can come against your confession of faith. And remember that your calling, like mine, is for confession. We are called to be proclaimers of the Word, preachers of the truth, and confessors of the gospel with our words and our lives.

6

Appointment and Disappointment

You've probably seen her or at least seen pictures of her. She sits on a prominent rocky point called Bennelong and, along with the Harbour Bridge, perfectly frames the gateway to downtown Sydney. She is the grand lady of the world's most stunning harbor. Her name is the Sydney Opera House, but her history is perhaps even rockier than the small peninsula on which she is built.

In 1956, a little-known Danish architect named Jorn Utzon entered a contest to design a significant building in a foreign city. His submission landed in the hands of four judges, who promptly discarded it into the pile of failed proposals. But the arrival of a fifth judge, renowned American architect Eero Saarinen, would change that forever. After seeing the shortlisted designs, Saarinen sought to examine the previously discarded entries, and he discovered the ambitious and unusual entry of Utzon. This design would go on to win the contest, and today it's his architectural masterpiece that crowns Bennelong Point in Sydney Harbour as one of the most iconic metropolitan structures in the world.[*]

To think that this remarkable and significant design once lay in a pile of rejected entries makes me wonder what other genius ideas have been overlooked. But the story does not end there.

Disappointment plagued the building of the opera house. Architect Jorn Utzon was confronted by huge amounts of criticism and experienced Australian cynicism at its worst. Amid a lack of both support and funds, and due to a discouraging game of political cat and mouse, Utzon wiped the dust from his shoes and walked off the job before the interior of his dream was ever completed. His name was not even mentioned during the opening ceremony. Bitterly disappointing.

It was more than forty years later when Utzon received a call from the newly elected New South Wales government requesting that he and his architect son return to Australia to redesign part of the interior of the famed building. He had begun to receive the recognition for his work that he deserved. And today his opera house remains iconic. In the words of architect Frank Gehry, "Utzon made a building well ahead of its time, far ahead of available technology, and he persevered through extraordinarily malicious publicity and negative criticism to build a building that changed the image of an entire country."[†]

From appointment to disappointment to appointment again. Ever experience anything like it?

---

[*] Anthony Burke, "A Danish Architect, an Australian Icon: The History of the Sydney Opera House," ABC, October 21, 2013, www.abc.net.au/news/2013-10-21/anthony-burke-on-sydney-opera-house-history/5034028.

[†] Frank Gehry, quoted in Eric Ellis, "Utzon Breaks His Silence," *Sydney Morning Herald,* September 16, 2014, www.smh.com.au/good-weekend/gw-classics/utzon-breaks-his-silence-20140904-10c93e.html.

God-Given Appointment

Each morning as I wake up, I know that if I were to open the calendar in my phone, I would see a well-organized list of appointments that will both start and end my day. Pastoral appointments, staff appointments, breakfast appointments, lunch appointments, family appointments, and of course everyone's least favorite, dentist appointments. My assistant, Megan, has been with me for twenty years, and I can count on her to keep my weekly appointments in timely order so as to fulfill all my obligations yet not stifle the spontaneous moments of life.

Appointments seem to be the streamline of life. I think even the structurally incompetent among us need to have the predictability of appointments.

Did you know that life is also full of God-appointments? Along with the dreams you have for your life, the calling and grace bestowed upon you, and the gifts within you, life is filled with situations and opportunities that were specifically chosen by God and planned before your first breath in order that you might fulfill the abundant purposes that you were destined for. John 15:16 says it clearly: "You did not choose Me, but I chose you and appointed you."

Throughout Scripture, we see appointment in various forms. Priests were appointed. Singers were appointed. Kings were appointed. Land was appointed. Governors were appointed. Entire people groups were appointed. And even days were appointed by God. But one such story that always comes back to me in moments of pondering appointment and all that comes along with it is that of Jeremiah.

Jeremiah recounts more of his own life than any other prophet in the Bible. We hear of his call to ministry, the reaction of his followers, his tests and trials, and everything from his inner struggles to his public speech. He was the son of a priest and from a small village just a few miles northeast of Jerusalem. His ministry spanned five decades, and he was a prophet to Israel during one of the darkest periods of their history. But it was his appointment by God that I think is both relatable and fascinating:

> The word of the LORD came to me, saying:
> "Before I formed you in the womb I knew you;
> Before you were born I sanctified you;
> I ordained you a prophet to the nations."

> Then said I:
> "Ah, Lord GOD!
> Behold, I cannot speak, for I am a youth."

> But the LORD said to me:
> "Do not say, 'I am a youth,'
> For you shall go to all to whom I send you,
> And whatever I command you, you shall speak.
> Do not be afraid of their faces,
> For I am with you to deliver you," says the LORD.

> Then the LORD put forth His hand and touched my mouth, and
> the LORD said to me:
> "Behold, I have put My words in your mouth.
> See, I have this day set you over the nations and over
>   the kingdoms,

> To root out and to pull down,
>
> To destroy and to throw down,
>
> To build and to plant." (Jeremiah 1:4–10)

Does Jeremiah's response to his God-appointment sound familiar? I think that, too often, even though we long for more, it is easy to be overwhelmed by it. Just as we discussed in previous chapters, the abundant blessings of God don't come without stretching and perhaps a bit of uncomfortable growth. Perhaps you too have made excuses when facing unknown, hard, or overwhelming tasks.

Self-disqualification. We've all done it—looked at our own inadequacies and tried to talk ourselves out of, or doubted, the very things we have heard God speak over us. You're in good company. Did you know that Moses did the same? So did Gideon.

Moses tried his hardest to get out of his assignment to speak with Pharaoh, saying, "I can't do it! I'm such a clumsy speaker! Why should Pharaoh listen to me?" (Exodus 6:30, NLT).

Perhaps the name Gideon isn't familiar to you. That's the point! Gideon was, in many ways, a nobody whom God called to be a somebody. He was going about his own business, threshing wheat for his father, when the Lord spoke to him about leading a risky military operation against the nation's enemies. And Gideon protested with several excuses as to why he could not rescue Israel as God had anointed him to: "Please, Lord, how can I save Israel? Behold, my clan is the weakest in Manasseh, and I am the least in my father's house" (Judges 6:15, ESV).

The dreams you have for your life, the calling and grace upon you, and the gifts within you are all perfectly lined up to fulfill your appointment. Just as God appointed Jeremiah as a prophet to the nations,

He has appointed you for a unique assignment and has ordained appointments for you along the way. No one can disqualify you from a God-appointment.

But life is unpredictable, and following God's call on our lives doesn't give us immunity from heartache, bumps in the road, and disappointment. Allow me to lead you through some of my own moments of disappointment and dissatisfaction—times when my faith has been tested. And discover with me how these momentary troubles can either derail our futures or propel us into our destinies.

Inevitable Disappointment

Sadly, disappointments are a part of life. We will all experience the pain of heartache, the disillusionment of relationship breakdown, and the reality of trust being shattered. Disappointment can immobilize us—the loss of a loved one or that sudden, inexplicable change that throws us off the path we were so certain was the will of God. I've shared extensively in my first book, *Live Love Lead,* how one of my life's greatest disappointments not only shattered my reality but had great consequences for my future. It would be true to say that in my sixty-three years of life, I have discovered that whenever you step out into God-appointment, it's incredible how often this sacrificial move is followed closely by disappointment. I am convinced that this very thing is a tactic of the devil to resist kingdom progress and discourage believers.

The day was a Saturday in late October. It was seven years after I had graduated Bible college and just a year or so into our marriage. Bobbie and I made the faith decision to step out in ministry. We moved from New Zealand to Sydney, New South Wales, and modest appointments began to come my way to speak in some of the most rural and unheard-of towns along the Australian east coast. We weren't going to be paid for our ministry, so to supplement our expenses, I was cleaning windows in a well-known shopping district named Paddington, near downtown Sydney. Bobbie was nineteen weeks pregnant with our first-born. We had just packed up our car for our first ministry trip to "the bush."

This car was the indestructible kind: a good Australian vehicle with four doors, a V-8 engine, and an oversized and reinforced bumper on the front that looked as though we could plow through any obstacle that got in our way. We had literally just pulled out of the driveway of our rented home and turned the corner when—*wham!*—we drove head-on into a little foreign sedan that seemed to come out of nowhere. Bobbie had been in the process of putting on her seat belt as we were moving, and at that exact moment she flew forward and hit her head squarely on the dash. The residents on that narrow street ran out to offer assistance and called an ambulance. We were thankful that, after the paramedics had checked her condition, the ambulance was not needed. True to form, our Transformer-like vehicle had barely a scratch, but the other driver's little two-door hatchback had folded like an accordion.

Fortunately, we were driving very slowly, and no one was significantly injured, but as we discovered later that day (in the days before I ever had staff or an assistant to help me with administrative tasks), I had somehow, in the busyness of life, allowed our automobile insurance to lapse. Crushing disappointment. Just as we had stepped out into the very thing we felt God had called and appointed us to, we were met with a huge blow to our resources and some time-consuming details to tend to.

Have you ever felt disappointed? I know you have. The prefix *dis* means to go in the other direction. To *dis*appoint is to be taken off course from what God has appointed you to do.

Dislike. Distrust. Disability. Disappointment. Disadvantage. Disagree. Disallow. Disbarred. Discord. Disconnect. Discontent. The list goes on.

God appoints us, and if we respond with disappointment, disagreement, discord, and the rest, it robs us, and we can draw back from what God has. And although it's true, just as the premise of this book states, that God has more for us than we could ever imagine, living above disappointment is a skill—a necessity—we need to grasp that abundant life.

Following Jeremiah's appointment, he too had a life that was plagued by disappointment. Even though he was faithful to the call on his life (he stepped into the work of a prophet, serving God and boldly declaring the word of the Lord), he saw no great revival. He didn't fill stadiums or draw large crowds, and the persecution he endured was crippling.

Jeremiah 20:1–2 documents the moment the chief governor in the house of the Lord struck Jeremiah and put him in stocks behind the high gate of the city. Confined to a degrading and public form of humiliation, Jeremiah cried out in the streets,

> You pushed me into this, GOD, and I let you do it.
> > You were too much for me.
> And now I'm a public joke.
> > They all poke fun at me.
> Every time I open my mouth
> > I'm shouting, "Murder!" or "Rape!"
> And all I get for my GOD-warnings
> > are insults and contempt. (verses 7–8, MSG)

Perhaps you find yourself in Jeremiah's shoes: disappointed with God, confused by your circumstances. You've followed the call of God on your life, only to discover roadblocks and heartache or pain at the hands of people who have continuously disappointed you. Maybe a miscarriage or a terminal diagnosis or an unexpected expense has blindsided you. Are you crying out like Jeremiah? Are you desperate for answers and hope and healing? Crying out to God is step one. But discovering what promises and truths are on the *inside* of you is what will really sustain you.

Never Wasted

Did you know that in the same way God uses the good things and the wise choices we make, nothing disappointing is ever wasted in the economy of God? It's true. No experience, not even a difficult one, is ever wasted if you use it wisely. God can use whatever you've been through and whatever comes up against you to develop you into the person He intended you to be.

Look at the life of Moses. He grew up in the home of his enemy. As the adopted son of Pharaoh's daughter, he spent forty years learning the language and ways of the Egyptians, the very people who persecuted his own family and an entire generation of Hebrews. What better preparation for understanding your adversary than being raised among them. And although Moses is often spoken of with great honor and respect for his righteousness, he learned some difficult and life-altering lessons through his personal failures.

Or maybe you are more like the apostle Paul. He was on his way to be a missionary in Spain but instead ended up in prison. Sitting in a

Roman jail, Paul must have thought a time or two, *Goodbye, appointment; hello, disappointment.*

Maybe you are in the "before more" stage of your life, feeling as though you are in a desert season tending sheep rather than in the powerful courts of the king or leading people into their freedom. Remember this: God never wastes an experience. He doesn't *cause* disappointment, but if you will allow your faith to be refined and choose to use wisely the time and opportunity in front of you, God will use it all for His good and His glory.

Forty years in a desert, tending sheep and wandering desolate places, prepared Moses for what was ultimately his destiny: to lead God's people through their own wilderness and toward *their* respective destinies.

And with an unexpected time in prison, Paul chose to write instead of worry. Because of that decision, we have the epistles to Philemon, the Colossians, the Philippians, and the Ephesians. Talk about turning disappointment into appointment!

Perhaps you too are wandering in a place where you would rather not be. If you are living in a disappointing or desert season or in what feels like the opposite of your abundant life, take heart: there are better days ahead.

You, right now, have a gift of time that can be used to fulfill God's purpose in your life. And you have opportunities and appointments in front of you that can lead you into the glorious destiny that awaits. There is wisdom in asking if you are stewarding your God-given days and opportunity as well as you can. Make the prayer of Psalm 90:12 your own:

> Teach us to number our days,
>   that we may gain a heart of wisdom. (NIVII)

Take it from Jeremiah. When he cried out to God out of desperation and disappointment, it wasn't his final confession.

Temporary Disappointment = Eternal Character

Live from the inside out rather than the outside in. Perhaps that is easier said than done, but what we discover through the life of Jeremiah is that what was *in* him was greater than any disappointment that came *against* him.

In Jeremiah 20:9, only *one verse* after the prophet shouts his disappointment at God, he says,

His word was in my heart like a burning fire
Shut up in my bones;
I was weary of holding it back,
And I could not.

To Jeremiah, silence was worse than suffering. He was compelled to follow God's call. He was convinced of his God-appointment and wouldn't let even the worst of pain and disappointment derail his opportunity.

Every challenge we face is an opportunity to challenge disappointment. It takes godly character to sustain that which God appoints. Regardless of your current circumstances, you are going to have to decide if what is burning in you is greater than the disappointment that is trying to rob you. Paul tells us,

Having been justified by faith, we have peace with God through our Lord Jesus Christ, through whom also we have access by faith into this grace in which we stand, and rejoice in hope of the glory of God. And not only that, but we also glory in tribulations, knowing that tribulation produces perseverance; and perseverance, character; and character, hope. Now hope does not disappoint, because the love of God has been poured out in our hearts by the Holy Spirit who was given to us. (Romans 5:1–5)

Tribulation, or what we're calling *disappointment,* produces perseverance, and perseverance, character. It is so easy to allow temporary disappointment to overrule God-given appointment, but don't do it! Take hold of the opportunity in front of you to produce in you a deep work, a sustaining harvest of patience, character, hope, and love.

Appointment Makes Room

The greater your character, the more God can pour into you. Many people take hold of God-given appointment with character that cannot sustain their roles. James 1:4 says, "Let perseverance finish its work so that you may be mature and complete, not lacking anything" (NIV11). We must allow God to teach us through our trials, test us through our tribulations, and develop us through our disappointments so that when the blessing comes, we are ready for it.

When God brings forth blessing, He doesn't just sprinkle it out; He pours it forth. Earlier in this chapter, I quoted John 15:16, which reads, "You did not choose Me, but I chose you and appointed you." But it doesn't finish there. The remainder of the verse says this: "that you should go and bear fruit, and that your fruit should remain, that whatever you ask the Father in My name He may give you."

Whatever you ask. The abundant fruitfulness of God. This is His will for your life and His purpose in your appointment.

As a young preacher traveling the back roads of New South Wales, showing up at meetings of five to a hundred people, I never could have imagined the roads we would take to get where we are now—roads that have been filled with miracles as much as with disappointments. When we started services in a little school hall in the suburbs of Sydney, I never could have imagined we would also be speaking weekly to large crowds in the center of São Paulo, Brazil. But that is precisely how our God operates.

Eugene Peterson's The Message puts it like this:

There's more to come: We continue to shout our praise even when we're hemmed in with troubles, because we know how troubles can develop passionate patience in us, and how that patience in turn forges the tempered steel of virtue, keeping us alert for whatever God will do next. In alert expectancy such as this, we're never left feeling shortchanged. Quite the contrary—we can't round up enough containers to hold everything God generously pours into our lives through the Holy Spirit! (Romans 5:3–5)

It's like the oil provided for the widow in the Old Testament (see 2 Kings 4:1–6). It's like the promise of poured-out blessing as we practice the discipline of tithing (see Malachi 3:10). The abundance of God is lavished upon us in ways that are greater, higher, and more exciting than we could imagine.

As I stand at a Sunday morning service in our Hills Campus, I am aware that simultaneously there are services taking place in multiple locations around Sydney, up and down the coast of Queensland, in four metropolis locations of Melbourne, on the small island of Tasmania, and most recently on the farthest northern coast, affectionately known to Australians as "the Top End," in the harbor port of Darwin. We can't round up enough containers.

Have there been disappointments along the way? You bet. Crushing disappointments. But we've never let disappointment lead us or rob us, and we've seen the fruit in more ways than we can put into words.

Oh, and wait! There is a postscript to my car-wreck story. I mentioned that my insurance had lapsed and that, because we were already on a shoestring budget, it looked as though we would have to withdraw from my humble preaching appointments in order to work for more money and pay for the car I had hit, which was a new and expensive model. But true to His nature, God came to my rescue in an almost unheard-of fashion. The manager of the insurance company came to interview me in our poky little one-bedroom apartment, and after hearing my story and glancing at my pregnant wife, he said, "I have never done this before, but because you are in ministry, even though your insurance is invalid, we will pay for the repairs." It was a huge confirmation that we were on the right path. When that man had left, I literally danced around the room, overjoyed at the faithfulness of God.

God *never* disappoints, my friend. He can do the same for you. And where He allows disappointment, He will forge in you the tempered steel of virtue, the passion of perseverance, and an alert expectancy for all that is ahead.

Corrie ten Boom has said, "When a train goes through a tunnel and it gets dark, you don't throw away your ticket and jump off. You sit still and trust the engineer."‡

God appoints, but He doesn't disappoint. You are called, saved, purposed, and graced for His appointment, and hope does not disappoint. Fate is not your portion. Failure is not your end. Instead, let hope be your beacon, faith be your compass, and purpose be your destination. On the way to more, bumps in the road are merely building your character and strengthening your testimony for the future that God has planned.

I'm known for this saying, and I will say it over and over again until it resonates in your soul, because, whether you believe it or not, *the best really is yet to come.*

I want to declare to you that no end is final, no failure is fatal, no mistake is unredeemable, and no life is unreachable. Whatever you are going through or have gone through doesn't disqualify you from the promise of God and the appointment that is in front of you. He came to give you a life filled with purpose, blessing, and more.

---

‡ Corrie ten Boom, *Jesus Is Victor* (Old Tappan, NJ: Revell, 1985), 183.

7

Ready and Receptive

Lexi Milan Houston—my third grandchild and the second-oldest daughter of my son Ben and his wife, Lucille. To describe Lexi as a lover of life would not do justice to the kind of enthusiastic, wide-eyed passion that daily exudes from this small but fierce human being. Lexi is something else. Like millions of little girls around the world, including her sisters, she will dance herself to exhaustion with very little inhibition.

It was exactly this zest for living that made her first visit to Disneyland so special, not only for her but also for me, her Pops, who on that particularly beautiful California afternoon was seeing the world through little Lexi's four-year-old eyes. It was then that I understood it was no wonder Jesus tells us in Scripture, "Assuredly, I say to you, unless you are converted and become as little children, you will by no means enter the kingdom of heaven. Therefore whoever humbles himself as this little child is the greatest in the kingdom of heaven" (Matthew 18:3–4). You open your eyes just that much wider when you see the world through a child's perspective. Like a sponge, absorbing every new experience the day presents, children take in more than their little minds can compute or their big eyes can conceive. Lexi's love for life was never more evident than that day, and Bobbie and I felt honored to be there.

Our night finished with the famous Disney parade, and we knew that all Lexi's favorites would no doubt be making an appearance—Mickey, Donald, and Goofy, yes, but it was all the princesses and the characters from *Frozen* that would be the icing on the cake. We lined up early—not something this sixty-three-year-old would normally do without a great deal of impatience. But this day was different. I was enjoying our Disney adventure through the eyes of a kid again, and it was a joy to behold as Lexi stood boldly among thousands, having claimed her spot next to the curb, where she screamed the name of every single Disney character who came past. "Donald Duck! Mickey! Ariel! Cinderella! Hi!" Her enthusiasm, excited voice, and occasional dance move meant that she regularly got eye contact, a huge smile, plus a big warm wave from each and every one of those legendary characters who have brought joy to millions. Even though she was one little girl among thousands, Lexi felt as though she were the only one there.

I think receptivity can do that. It can open doors that have you feeling like one in a thousand, maybe even one in a million. Now, is that an exaggeration? Not necessarily. "Exceedingly, abundantly above" is God's promise when He is the power that works within us.

Lexi's receptivity opened doors for her as one by one her heroes walked by and engaged with her wonder-filled fantasy. I believe that when you live your life alert, alive, present, and receptive, that is exactly what wide-eyed wonder will do for you, too! It will open doors of opportunity and enable you to see what you may have otherwise missed. Rather than letting important voices become background noise, you can begin to hear what you need to.

The Power of Receptivity

Jesus often said, "If anyone has ears to hear, let him hear" (Mark 4:23). On one such occasion, He went on to say to His disciples, "Take heed what you hear. With the same measure you use, it will be measured to you; and to you who hear, more will be given" (verse 24).

One of my many weaknesses lies in my ability to zone out in the middle of a conversation and get lost in my thoughts. At times I can be oblivious to those around me. There have been many times when one of my kids would be calling me as I watched the television news, and although I could hear her, it wouldn't register. My daughter, Laura, would be calling, "Dad . . . Daaad . . . *Dad!*" Then in frustration she would change tack and shout, "Brian!" at which I would swing around and ask her what she wanted. Not a good habit, I know.

But how wide eyed, how alert, how switched on are you to the world around you? If the Holy Spirit is speaking to you, do you have the ears to hear His whisper, or would you not hear Him even if His whisper became a shout? Life itself presents us all with so many distractions, worries, and concerns that can fill up our hearts, block our ears, and dim our vision. The noise of life can so easily drown out what God is trying to say.

I believe that when Jesus was speaking to His disciples about "measure" in Mark 4:24, He was indicating that so often a sense of complacency and our inability to hear can rob us of the measure God intends when it comes to fulfilling His promises in our lives.

What awakens in you the simplicity of a little child? What sparks that innocent faith that the circumstances of life can rob from you? Do you have a vision exciting enough to get you up early, or a dream inspiring enough to bring anticipation so deep down in your soul that it makes you smile every time you are reminded of it? Are you ready for more? What I mean by that is, have you prepared yourself for all that God has planned for your future? It's a big question and perhaps followed promptly by, well, what *does* God have for your future? I may not be able to answer that specifically for you, but what I hope you have determined from this book already is that He has good plans, big plans. He knows your heart's desires and is poised to fulfill them, but are you ready to receive?

Perhaps you believe you are past all that now. You have become a "realist" and are settled into living quietly for the Lord and placing all your expectation in spending eternity in His presence. If that is the truth, then I say it's a pity, because no one is saved for heaven alone. Praise God that heaven is our final reward, but you are saved, called, purposed, and graced to make a difference here on earth *now,* among your friends, family, neighbors, and coworkers and through every opportunity God brings your way. Yes, Jesus died to save you from your sins, but He also died to bring heaven to earth and for you and me to live surrendered to His cause. If you lose sight of the "more" the apostle Paul speaks of in Ephesians 3:20 (NIVII), you will become familiar, jaded, and perhaps even critical and cynical, which is no way for anyone to live!

In Acts 13, Paul speaks directly to people with that attitude:

Watch out, cynics;
Look hard—watch your world fall to pieces.
I'm doing something right before your eyes
That you won't believe, though it's staring you in the
> face. (verse 41, MSG)

Without receptivity, you can live just like this. Things can be staring you in the face that you just can't see. Familiarity and presumption will rob you of wonder, and cynicism or lack of expectancy will keep you from the more that God has for you.

Enemies to Receptivity

"The search for a 'suitable' church makes the man a critic where the Enemy wants him to be a pupil," says C. S. Lewis in *The Screwtape Letters*. "What He wants from the layman in church is an attitude which may, indeed, be critical in the sense of rejecting what is false or unhelpful, but which is wholly uncritical in the sense that it does not appraise—does not waste time in thinking about what it rejects, but lays itself open in uncommenting, humble receptivity to any nourishment that is going."*

Lewis could be talking about the kind of attitudes that are so prevalent not only in our churches but also in our families and our homes. It's easy to become a critic—to complain about the traffic in the parking lot and the loud music, to criticize our spouse or find fault with our children. But criticism will only harden your heart to what God longs to show you. Hurt and pain lock you out of being open and accessible. Avoiding forgiveness and allowing bitterness to take root will cause negativity to drown out receptivity.

The apostle Paul hailed the Macedonian believers and churches as examples of immense openness and generosity. Their circumstances were extreme, as deep recession and a dire financial crisis had taken hold in their region, but look at their inspiring example that Paul shared with the

---

* C. S. Lewis, *The Screwtape Letters: Annotated Edition* (1942; reprint and annotation, San Francisco: HarperOne, 2013), 94.

Corinthian church: "We make known to you the grace of God bestowed on the churches of Macedonia: that in a great trial of affliction the abundance of their joy and their deep poverty abounded in the riches of their liberality" (2 Corinthians 8:1–2).

Note the two qualities that verse 2 speaks of: the "abundance of their joy" and the "riches of their liberality." Their beautiful receptivity and openness to God meant that they did not allow their situation to diminish the undeniable joy and generosity that trademarked these Macedonian believers.

As a pastor, I have witnessed this many times over the years: the first two things that disappear when something has changed in the heart of an individual, a couple, or perhaps a family are joy and generosity. Their countenance changes. People begin to draw back; they are not the open books they used to be, for while they are still present, they no longer seem to be "there." The generous words, the encouraging smiles, and the willing giving both of time and finances dry up. The readiness has gone, the receptivity is no more, and (inwardly, at least) they have checked out.

Was it a hurt or offense? Has someone done something to them, or have they taken on board the offense or opinion of others? Or perhaps they have simply left what the Bible refers to as their "first love" (their relationship with God) and allowed their circumstances to jade the way they view the world and have let their hearts grow cold. Many things can take root in your heart or mine if we do not diligently protect it.

In the same way that an unprotected heart stifles receptivity, familiarity can breed contempt, and mediocrity quickly becomes bondage. Matthew 13:57–58 describes how Jesus was a familiar face in His hometown. People simply thought of him as "the carpenter's son" (verse 55), and it was because of their perception that they were offended by the words He spoke and the truth He told. "Jesus said to them, 'A prophet is not without honor except in his own country and in his own house.' Now He did not do many mighty works there because of their unbelief" (verses 57–58). It would be true to say that their familiarity locked God out of His own home. Because of their unbelief, Jesus did not do miracles there, and they missed out on what could have been.

The same thing can happen to us if we limit God through our lack of receptivity by becoming too familiar with what He has to offer. Perhaps you're thinking, *Yeah, but my life is filled with the familiar.* Maybe you would even call your weekly routine mundane. I understand the daily grind of getting up, working, providing for your family, and coming home to pay the bills and put the kids to bed. I also have come to understand that God is in the details. The smallest detail and seemingly ordinary grind of our daily lives doesn't go unnoticed or unrewarded by Him. Faithfulness in the little things—doing daily, ordinary life well—is crucial to experiencing the more that God promises. Don't be discouraged by what seems ordinary, and don't allow familiarity to rob you of a God encounter.

Can I encourage you? Don't allow offense, familiarity, or mediocrity to take you on a journey away from the purposes of God.

So, what does familiarity look like?

As young pastors, Bobbie and I were invited to Perth, a five-hour flight from one side of the world's largest island continent to the other. Our hosts and new friends, Phil and Heather, picked us up, and we were overawed when we arrived at the beautiful hotel where they had arranged for us to be accommodated. We had never been in such a beautiful hotel before, and everything in our room was so wonderful! Every towel was perfectly positioned, the bed had what seemed like a dozen pillows, the television was bigger than the one we had at home, and there were a hundred little details that had us feeling overwhelmed that our friends would spoil us in such a way. We really were surprised and so grateful to God for His goodness.

Fast-forward a number of years, and I found myself speaking at the same church and staying in the same hotel. But something had changed. Once checked in, I raced to the room, threw my case on the bed, and then caught myself inwardly complaining about a detail I wasn't happy about. It was in that moment that I suddenly stopped and remembered how just a decade before, I had been so grateful to be with Bobbie in such a fine hotel. What had changed? I had become used to the blessing, and familiarity had taken hold. I certainly checked myself then and there because I never want to become familiar with the blessings of God and the kindness of others. I realize that familiarity opposes the open stance in life that has us ready and poised for all that God brings our way.

You too can become familiar with God's blessing and overfamiliar with your job, your ministry, your opportunity, your friends, or your church. Perhaps you already have. You know, it's when the worship does not move you anymore and you just don't sense God's presence the way you once did. It's when your pastor's preaching doesn't feed you the way it used to or when the sense of family and your appreciation for the church community you are a part of wanes. Maybe you find that during conversations, you highlight the negatives and forget the blessing your own local church has been in your life. Familiarity has you believing that it's not you but the church that's changed. It seems to you that the worship isn't as good as it used to be and the pastor has lost his edge. You've heard it all before, and you are looking for something more. When this is the case, God has so much more for you, but familiarity is distancing you from His will and purpose in your life. Perhaps it's not the pastor, the worship, or the church that has changed. Perhaps the shift is in you.

When familiarity pervades the congregation in any church, momentum is stalled, spontaneity disappears, the community seems less loving, and the altars are empty. The worship becomes mechanical, and the message no longer penetrates the hardened hearts of the congregation. Maybe you think that all seems overdramatic, but I promise you, it's not. Openness, spiritual hunger, gratitude, and receptivity are attributes of a healthy church, and every one of us has our part to play in that.

Playing Your Part

Look at this wonderful picture of the gathering of God's people in an open square in Israel. It's recorded in Nehemiah 8, and it is an amazing narrative on receptivity. The Jerusalem wall had been rebuilt according to God's instructions and with Nehemiah's leadership. During the Feast of Tabernacles, the people had built a wooden platform in preparation for Ezra the priest to read the law. As a big crowd gathered in that open square, and as Ezra stood on the temporary timber platform, he opened the Torah. Look at the amazing response of the people:

> Ezra opened the book in the sight of all the people, for he was standing above all the people; and when he opened it, all the people stood up. And Ezra blessed the LORD, the great God.
>
> Then all the people answered, "Amen, Amen!" while lifting

up their hands. And they bowed their heads and worshiped the
LORD with their faces to the ground. (verses 5–6)

What a picture! All Ezra did was open the book, and a chorus rang
out with people shouting in one accord, "Amen, Amen!" with their
hands in the air. Then, with heads bowed and faces to the ground, they
worshipped the Lord. That is a pretty enthusiastic crowd! The atmosphere was charged with praises. Receptivity does that for you. It not only
opens doors but also charges the atmosphere, bringing that sense that
anything could happen and it probably will.

How can we recapture this enthusiasm in our worship today?

I know the difference wide-eyed receptivity brings to the atmosphere
of a church service—I can feel it. When people lean in to the worship
and are hungry for the Word, preaching is a joy. The atmosphere brings
greater clarity to my mind. My words have a flow, and the presence of the
Holy Spirit is evident when people are ready to receive. That's what I
mean by a "charged atmosphere." It's tangible, it's powerful, it's beautiful
in its unity, and it's magnetic to newcomers. But the opposite is also true,
as a tired crowd who are there but not there, hearing but not hearing, will
have you feeling like Jesus's hometown crowd had Him feeling: a prophet
without honor in His own town (see Mark 6:4). Jesus could do no miracles there.

Have the miracles dried up in your life, and have you asked yourself
why? Perhaps you need a revival in your soul and a renewed approach to
life and living. Maybe you need to ask God to reignite the fire you once
had for the things of God. Invite Him to develop in you a hunger and
thirst for Scripture and a passion for life. Maybe you need a new sense of
urgency about matters of the kingdom, a bit like these guys . . .

Tear Off the Roof

I can just picture it. They knew what was going on inside that house. People were spilling out into the streets and whispering "It's a miracle!" and "Did you see him get healed?" They knew that the rabbi inside the house wasn't just an ordinary man. He was the one the whole countryside was talking about: Jesus.

They knew that this was their chance—the opportunity their friend needed. Their expectations were high, and their willingness to make it happen was buoyed by the similar attitude of their mates. But the crowd was too thick, so no one was willing to give up a spot, even for the man they carried, who had obvious infirmities. So they glanced up to the roof, and without saying a word, they knew what they had to do. They hoisted their paralyzed friend onto his mat and up on their shoulders. Digging through the hardened clay surface until their fingers were raw, they knew what could happen if they could just get their friend into that crowded room with Jesus (see Mark 2:1–5).

In the same way, filled with eager anticipation, someone else was being ministered to by the Son of God. Zacchaeus was the town tax collector, probably a corrupt and unlikable character, and the Bible tells us he was a man of small stature. Yet his hunger to see Jesus, his interest, and his wide-eyed receptivity to the message caused him to climb a tree and draw the attention of the Son of Man. "And when Jesus came to the place, He looked up and saw him, and said to him, 'Zacchaeus, make haste and come down, for today I must stay at your house.' So he made haste and came down, and received Him joyfully" (Luke 19:5–6).

Do you think Jesus is attracted by our desperate determination? I think that determination and a receptive posture will always attract miracles. Jesus Himself was often compelled by people's hunger and moved by those who sought after Him with expectancy for a life-changing encounter.

Do you live with wide-eyed anticipation? With the eagerness of a child about to receive a reward or enter the gates of Disneyland for the first time? Do you approach your relationship with Christ with the same purpose as Zacchaeus and the determination of the paralytic's friends? Do you still have expectation for the miraculous, desperation to receive from Jesus, and a heart that is ready? It's a challenge to us all, because there are so many obstacles in our daily lives that can hinder our being ready and receptive to all that God has.

Desire Greater Than Obstacles

When you live with receptivity, your desire will be greater than the obstacles. A phenomenon began in the late 1990s at our original Hillsong Campus in Sydney's Hills District, northwest of the city. We were in our first building, but it was significantly smaller than our growing congregation needed. So every Sunday, while one service was in progress, people would line up around the building, waiting patiently for the next service to begin. Believe me, in secular Australia, where people have an image of church being old, boring, empty, and irrelevant, it is not normal to see people lining up to get into church.

This same activity is now a feature of Hillsong churches in cities as diverse as Barcelona, Cape Town, London, Los Angeles, and New York City, where perhaps it's been taken to another level. People will line up around the block for an hour or more before church begins, eager to get inside. Freezing temperatures and scorching heat don't seem to deter the hundreds of people who faithfully and patiently wait for a seat in a Sunday service. Amazing!

Like at most churches, at Hillsong the Easter season is a very special time. It is our biggest weekend of the year, and after all our campuses have filled auditoriums, overflows, and any other available space for Good Friday and Resurrection Sunday morning services, people travel into Sydney's downtown, where for years we have seen thousands pack into an arena on Easter Sunday night. In 2014, we had just too many people arrive to hear evangelist Reinhard Bonnke speak. Thousands of people were left outside but didn't want to miss out, even though the weather report predicted heavy rain. And oh, did it rain! But within a few minutes of the service starting inside, it became apparent that the crowd waiting outside wasn't prepared to leave. They wanted to celebrate the resurrection of Christ too!

Due to some preplanning, quick thinking, and servant-hearted team members, by the time the third song was being sung inside, provision had been made for a huge overflow crowd outside. Many having donned makeshift raincoats, umbrellas, and plastic ponchos, they worshipped on and on, even after the service inside the arena was finally over. They were ready and receptive, and no obstacle would deter them as they engaged through ginormous screens that streamed the service in the pouring rain. It is my belief that their desperation to meet with God did not go unmet that Easter evening.

Similarly, it brings to mind times past when I have traveled with Hillsong United in South America. More than once, huge soccer stadiums in places such as Bogotá, Colombia, and Buenos Aires, Argentina, were thronging with people waiting to worship, but rain threatened to ruin the party. I never will forget the intensity and perseverance as up to seventy thousand people worshipped, faces toward heaven, arms stretched high, tears in so many eyes, even though many were standing ankle deep in muddy puddles and soaked to the bone by unrelenting rain. Even as I preached the message of Jesus Christ, the crowds stood motionless, intently taking in every word. It certainly took "singing in the rain" to new levels.

Are you like those people? When was the last time you arrived at church with that kind of anticipation? Or were you ticked off when you arrived last week and discovered that you had to park far away from the entrance? Perhaps you came early, only to find that people had already saved the best seats. Or maybe you walked in and didn't recognize the person leading worship, didn't sing any songs you were familiar with, or had heard something uncomplimentary about the speaker that week. But did you lean in and learn anyway?

I'm the first to admit it's not always easy to maintain enthusiastic passion. But the power of receptivity can make all the difference to just how open heaven seems to be.

Please don't get me wrong here. The Christian life is not a constant happy-clappy experience. I know as well as anyone that there are many valley moments, hurts and worries, suffering and disappointments that can steal our joy and dampen our zeal. But acknowledging your suffering is not the same as wallowing in it. There is so much to be said for the person whose resolve is to remain soft and purehearted, eager to learn from tragedy and able to find God in suffering.

In your petition to God for more responsibility and blessing in the future, are you living eager, responsible and receptive to all the things He has brought into your life *now*?

Open Doors

We were in beautiful Fiji. The anticipation was palpable. The hot and humid little chapel was thick with excitement and eagerness. Every seat was occupied with a smiling face, taking in the beauty of the surroundings but equally enthusiastic about what was about to take place. As the bridegroom stood there, buttoned up in casual elegance, the smile on his face was shadowed only by the tears in his eyes. His heart was beating so fast that he was sure the entire island could hear. When the doors opened, it was as if the entire room breathed a sigh of elation, recognizing the weight of that moment. I will never forget the tangible feeling of love and anticipation that blanketed the room as I walked my only daughter, Laura, down the aisle of that chapel to her waiting Fijian groom. The moment we rounded the corner and could see down the short aisle, Laura and I both melted into tears. It is surely a parent's proudest moment.

I love this picture of receptivity. Peter would never have rejected Laura in that moment simply because perhaps he didn't like her dress or was offended if she were a few minutes late to the ceremony. No, instead he waited, anticipating the moment when those doors would open, confident of the gift clinging to my arm that I was about to give: his beautiful bride. And when those doors did open, his whole being lit up with excitement, relief, and passion for the one he loved, expected, and waited for.

Do you live with a similar anticipation for what God is about to do in your life? For the doors to open to the next opportunity, blessing, and provision from Him? Are you confident in the beauty that awaits you? If you don't live with anticipation, you can miss out on what God intends. What is your expectation? What are you believing for this year, in your life and in the lives of those around you? Are you waiting on God with the same wide-eyed anticipation as that of an eager groom? Receptivity opens doors: "Ask, and it will be given to you; seek, and you will find; knock, and it will be opened to you. For everyone who asks receives, and he who seeks finds, and to him who knocks it will be opened" (Matthew 7:7–8). What a promise!

Our receptivity opens us to so much more possibility. Let's decide that we want to live in such a way as to not miss any opportunity. Let's live with intention, free from distraction, and aware of the abundant potential there is in Christ.

Pay Attention

It's all about paying attention. Attention brings retention—you can't retain what you don't contain. For example, if I'm not listening to you, I won't understand what you're saying! We need to have our hearts' attention consistently attuned to God and our souls constantly fed from His Word.

From retention comes intention, and from intention comes conception. Now that you have the Word inside you and you're hearing the voice of God, it should invoke a response. And from that response, you are now in a place to conceive—to birth new things and see further ahead into the future with hope and anticipation. See? So much potential comes from simply paying attention.

What is it that you need to pay attention to in order to birth new things in your life? Don't rob yourself and others by not regularly receiving the Word of God or by flirting with mediocrity or contempt. Isaiah says this:

Have you not known?
Have you not heard?
Has it not been told you from the beginning?
Have you not understood from the foundations of the earth?
It is He who sits above the circle of the earth,
And its inhabitants are like grasshoppers,
Who stretches out the heavens like a curtain,
And spreads them out like a tent to dwell in. . . .

Lift up your eyes on high,
And see who has created these things,
Who brings out their host by number;
He calls them all by name,
By the greatness of His might
And the strength of His power;
Not one is missing. (Isaiah 40:21–22, 26)

You're robbing yourself of potential and robbing others by not paying attention and receiving. It is paramount on this journey toward discovering more of who God is and more of what He has for you that you keep your heart uncritical, be attentive, and absorb the Word of God and the miracles every day. Be appreciative, because thanksgiving comes before the miraculous. Take what you hear, apply it to your life, and get ready! The same God who calls the stars by name is preparing to write an epic tale on the pages of your life, if you would only be ready to receive.

8

Credibility and Consistency

Spectacular homes and elaborate marketplaces and arenas dotted the ancient city of Pompeii. Upper-class Roman citizens flocked to this distinguished cultural hub that flourished with all kinds of trades and art. Painstakingly established in the sixth century BC, this masterful and modern city took years to build but only moments to destroy when volcanic ash from the unexpected eruption of Mount Vesuvius buried the city and many of the people who dwelled there.

The Golden Gate Bridge, an icon of San Francisco that rises above its famous bay, took four years and $35 million to build in the 1930s. Experts estimate that with major seismic activity, it would take sixty seconds to crumble.

It takes a long time to build a life—years of consistency, faithfulness, longevity, and other unglamorous or even boring old-fashioned virtues. It's the credibility you build over your entire lifetime—a platform of long-term trust building, carved out in authenticity—that becomes your proving ground. In turn, this authenticity produces great fruit as you keep on keeping on. And to think that all of it can be destroyed in the blink of an eye, like with the tragedy of Vesuvius.

Thankfully, no sin, failure, or mistake is unredeemable. But the devastation, humiliation, pain, and sheer futility of destroyed credibility is something I have witnessed far too often in my years of leading the Australian Christian Churches, a movement of more than eleven hundred churches in our nation. I have experienced the pain of sitting across the desk from a fallen leader who is doubled over with remorse, regret, and heartbroken repentance. It is not an experience I welcome or look forward to, for obvious reasons. It's painful to witness the tragedy of a devastated spouse or a family thrown into crisis, or the groaning sound as someone wakes to the realization of what he has destroyed and reflects on what might have been.

That said, I believe there is always a path back because of the forgiving and restorative nature of God and His grace. But it is the bedrock of credibility that is lost in the eyes of other people, in particular the people who have been betrayed, that creates long-term damage. There's always a way back through repentance and changed behavior, but when credibility is lost, it can be a long, difficult, and painful journey.

The Blessing of Authenticity, Credibility, and Consistency

Significant keys to God's doing more than you could ever ask, think, or imagine are authenticity, credibility, and consistency. These play vital parts in the journey to the exponential nature of God's blessing, the shake-your-head-in-disbelief kind of blessing that is carved out through keeping your course.

The journey that Bobbie and I have enjoyed has seen blessing ramp up as the years have gone by, each decade disproportionate to the ten years that preceded it. God's measure is so different from ours. Many times I've pondered this promise:

A day in Your courts is better than a thousand.
I would rather be a doorkeeper in the house of my God
Than dwell in the tents of wickedness. (Psalm 84:10)

One day better than a thousand! Could God possibly do in one day what once would take a thousand days? I know He can. I've seen it in my own pastoral journey. The number of people we were able to reach in any given week in our pioneering days in 1983 was less than a hundred. Now, with the help of facilities, technology, vision, and a heart for mission that has continued to grow, we can communicate and do in a single day what would have taken a thousand before. And what is the secret? It's always a story of God's grace, but I believe it is also a consistent testimony and the fruit of credibility that has seen our reach accelerate and soar.

At the end of 2016, as Russian and Syrian bombs rained down on Aleppo, the suffering and desperation we saw through our television screens was unimaginable. Streams of children (many of whom had been orphaned), families left homeless, and individuals left without families fled for their lives with nothing more than their raggedy clothes as winter bore down on them. But a rallying call to our ever-generous congregations meant that on a single weekend, we were able to raise vastly more support than we ever could have thought more than thirty years ago. By the grace of God and through partnership with charity workers who risk their lives to bring physical and spiritual assistance to this war-torn nation, we were able to send hundreds of thousands of dollars right to the places where the money mattered most.

That's a testimony to the power of longevity. It's a story that would not be possible without the kind of credibility that over years has built the level of trust and consistency that inspires people to invest. Credibility is underrated. So too is authenticity. Our ability to make that impact was worth the daily grind of faithfulness, often borne out in the mundane and the unseen of everyday living rather than the glamor and highly visible big occasions and special days.

People will invest their time, energy, and resources in your vision if they trust you, believe in your cause, and witness your consistency. Authenticity is attractive. Not perfect, but genuine. Not infallible, but credible.

I know that this can be your story too. What may have taken you a decade will be accomplished in ever-quickening time when God is building your life and you are cooperating with His master plan through faithfulness and consistency.

A Certain Disciple

Timothy is a fitting example of faithfulness. This young man was chosen by the legendary apostle Paul to serve, lead, and travel right alongside him. Wow, what an opportunity! Why Timothy? Who was Timothy? How did he qualify for selection? Was it his New Testament version of an Ivy League education or his obvious oratory skills? The answer is perhaps a little less impressive. It seems his credibility and proven consistency may have been the key contributors.

The incredible relationship dynamic between the apostle Paul and the young disciple Timothy is a wonderful study. There is no doubt that their relationship was not only unique but anointed, ordained, and for kingdom purpose.

Even after all these years, when I read the Word of God, I find new revelation as my love for His Word has only grown. That is what happens when you read a living book. Searching the infinite treasures of God's immutable and unchangeable Word is a joy and privilege I don't take for granted. My personal study of the missionary journeys recorded in the book of Acts led me to a recent series of sermons I taught on Paul's early travels with his novice companion. It was in this study that the qualities of Timothy struck me as a rich lesson. I read the passages and found myself focused on the nuances of the text. Take a look at this one: "He came to Derbe and Lystra. And behold, a certain disciple was there, named Timothy, the son of a certain Jewish woman who believed, but his father was Greek. He was well spoken of by the brethren who were at Lystra and Iconium. Paul wanted to have him go on with him" (16:1–3).

Did you catch it? "And behold, a *certain* disciple was there, named Timothy, the son of a *certain* Jewish woman who believed, but his father was Greek."

What a strange way to describe someone—but it's not accidental. I think the author of Acts was trying to communicate something profound. This was not just "another" Timothy or "some" Jewish woman's son; he was handpicked by the legendary apostle with a sense of certainty. It was an assurance that Timothy was God's choice to be Paul's young ministry accomplice and traveling companion on his next missionary adventure, a journey that was not for the fainthearted. No summer vacation or sightseeing tour here. This was a rigorous trip fraught with perils and well recorded in the writings of Luke and Paul. I love the idea that this young man and even his family were set apart for the task Christ was calling them to, chosen long before Paul ever asked.

I believe the same could be said about you. And before we dive further into this chapter and focus on the imperative qualities that make a way for one's calling, I want to remind you of God's certainty when He chose you, formed you, and called you into His glorious light. It is with certainty that God saves, calls, purposes, and graces each one of us.

Whatever it is you feel on your heart to accomplish or the divine planting you are currently living, God was confident when He called you. Romans 11:29 says, "God's gifts and his call are irrevocable" (NIVII). In other words, they are final, unchanging, and *certain*. Again, it's as it was with the prophet Jeremiah:

> Before I formed you in the womb I knew you;
> Before you were born I sanctified you;
> I ordained you a prophet to the nations. (Jeremiah 1:5)

I don't think it would be amiss to also mention that Timothy was *chosen* by God and *picked* by Paul likely because of his servant heart and willing character. Service and sacrifice rarely go unnoticed.

A Genuine Faith

What does it mean to have a genuine faith? Have you ever heard someone described as a "real Christian"? I long to be a real Christian. I want people who might see me as "that Hillsong pastor" to also know me to be generous, kind, patient, loving, and Christlike off the platform: in my local coffee shop, at the gas station, or stuck in traffic. I'm afraid that sometimes I fail the fruit-of-the-Spirit test. What about you?

Paul came to the town of Lystra looking for young Timothy. The verses we've explored tell us that Timothy was well spoken of in his hometown. Both the book of Acts and the letters of Timothy paint a picture of this young disciple as a loyal follower, a wide-eyed learner, a young (but not novice) leader, and a trustworthy son with a credible platform. Additionally, Timothy would eventually become the pastor of the church in Ephesus—not a small platform either! We don't know the exact number of people he reached, but many would say that the Ephesian church attracted thousands and produced all manner of ministries.

Without a doubt, Timothy's success was directly linked to his character. Paul sought out this young disciple because of his integrity. In fact, the very first words recorded in Paul's first letter to Timothy are these: "To Timothy, a *true* son in the faith: Grace, mercy, and peace from God our Father and Jesus Christ our Lord" (1 Timothy 1:2). Paul was no doubt referring to Timothy's character as the real thing, genuine and unblemished. I believe that it is the will of God for you and me to also live true—true to ourselves, true in our relationships, true to our leadership and calling.

Matthew 7:15–20 in The Message says this: "Be wary of false preachers who smile a lot, dripping with practiced sincerity. Chances are they are out to rip you off some way or other. Don't be impressed with charisma; look for character. Who preachers *are* is the main thing, not what they say." In this passage, Jesus was pointing to the hypocrisy of the Pharisees. Throughout the Gospels, we see that these men of religion were not true to whom they were. More often than not, they would say one thing and do another.

Have you ever been hurt by someone like that? Hypocrisy hurts the church. It damages the bride of Christ and disillusions genuine followers of Jesus. And we are all guilty of it at some level or another. But the life of Timothy is an example to follow. His authenticity is what attracted Paul to him, and it opened doors of opportunity for him.

As an aside, let me caution you not to put pastors, teachers, and leaders on a pedestal. The Bible says in James 3:1 that teachers will be judged more strictly for what comes out of their mouths, but leave that to God and don't place expectations on them that you don't have of yourself.

Bobbie recalls one of the early days of Hillsong Church when we met in a school hall. Several families diligently set up the chairs and stage each week while many of the team prepped and prayed for the service out back. On that day as I walked into the auditorium just moments before the service was about to start, one of the young children, who had been patiently waiting while his parents served, sighed loudly and remarked, "Oh, thank goodness, we can start now—God's here!"

The concept of that moment makes me smile (if I were God, we would all be in a lot of trouble!), but far too many people hang their hopes on the example of a leader, the life of another flawed human being, elevating that person to a much higher position than they ought. And though it is biblical that leaders should be above reproach (see 1 Timothy 3:2), too much division throughout the years has been caused by the fall of shepherds or pastors who failed to meet expectations or, worse, lost their way themselves. The truth is, we are all called, anointed, and vital to the body of Christ. We all have a part to play and a burden to carry that requires loyalty, sincerity, authenticity, and genuine faith.

Great things happen when we live from a place of authenticity. I can testify to it. Timothy's attitude opened him to an unbelievable opportunity to learn from the best of the best. Paul poured himself into Timothy, and for that we have so much to be grateful for, because Timothy's genuine faith brought life to the early church.

Unqualified

Here's another step in Timothy's progress to productive servant of God:

> Paul wanted to have him go on with him. And he took him
> and circumcised him because of the Jews who were in that region,
> for they all knew that his father was Greek. And as they went
> through the cities, they delivered to them the decrees to keep,
> which were determined by the apostles and elders at Jerusalem.
> So the churches were strengthened in the faith, and increased in
> number daily. (Acts 16:3–5)

Perhaps it seems odd for Paul to share such intimate details as Timothy's circumcision with all future generations! But his recording of these events was not without reason.

Has anyone told you that you aren't up to scratch? That you don't fit, don't make the grade, or are unqualified? Maybe you've disqualified yourself. Perhaps you feel as though your past automatically dismisses you from opportunities that others have. This is the beauty of the gospel and the specialty of our Savior. No one is dismissed, not even the uncircumcised son of a Greek man moving in Jewish circles.

This was a line in the sand, a stake in the ground. Timothy was considered a Jew because of his Jewish mother, but if he remained uncircumcised, his ministry would prove a stumbling block to nearly every

Jew he would encounter. It was for the sake of the gospel that Timothy underwent this painful ritual in order that he might not disqualify himself from that which Christ had called him to.

On our road to discovering what God has for us, we will all undoubtedly come up against moments of doubt, discouragement, and intimidation. It is inevitable when gaining influence and making an impact. Yet Paul instructs us, the same way he instructed Timothy:

> Let no one despise your youth, but be an example to the believ-
> ers in word, in conduct, in love, in spirit, in faith, in purity. Till
> I come, give attention to reading, to exhortation, to doctrine.
> Do not neglect the gift that is in you, which was given to you
> by prophecy with the laying on of the hands of the eldership.
> Meditate on these things; give yourself entirely to them, that
> your progress may be evident to all. Take heed to yourself and
> to the doctrine. Continue in them, for in doing this you will save
> both yourself and those who hear you. (1 Timothy 4:12–16)

Serving God can become a lot of things. Paul was exhorting Timothy in this moment to be certain of the God call on his life, when there were all sorts of pressures and reasons to be uncertain. His age, his lack of experience, others' opinions, and worries could all so easily distract Timothy from what he was there for. But Paul was in effect saying, "Keep the main thing the main thing. Don't let intimidation determine your power. Don't let people treat lightly the gift that is in you. Let your example do the talking."

I love this last point. Did you know that there is not even one recorded sentence of Timothy's in the Bible? That's right—we never hear him speak! But Timothy doesn't need to say anything, because his *life* does the talking. Could the same be said about you?

Don't be halfhearted in your personal development. When Paul told Timothy to give attention to reading, exhortation, and doctrine, he was really saying, "Pay attention and devote yourself to your studies." In the same way, don't neglect the God deposit in your life. Commit yourself to reading the Word, and plant yourself in the house of God, where you can learn, grow, and be encouraged by other believers.

Paul finishes by telling Timothy to be kind to himself, basically saying, "Take care of the people I have entrusted to you and take care of yourself." Longevity requires that we look after ourselves. Years ago, I learned that Mr. Invincible doesn't exist. I am not indestructible, and in order to fulfill my role as a pastor, husband, father, and friend, I too need to "take heed to myself." What about you?

Don't allow others to disqualify you from the path you are destined to take. And in the same way, be careful not to disqualify yourself by making poor choices. Remember, leaders don't always *look* like leaders. I've always felt compelled to take a risk on people who to others may seem unqualified, because I feel like that's what God has always done with me. Look for credibility and authenticity—you can't manufacture that.

The Platform of Faithfulness

Meditate on Deuteronomy 1:11 with me for just a moment: "May the LORD God of your fathers make you a thousand times more numerous than you are, and bless you as He has promised you!"

This prayer, spoken by Moses to the children of Israel, was for a thousand-times blessing: more children, more fruitfulness than they could ever imagine. Can God breathe that level of increase into your dreams? I have no doubt He can, if your dreams are built on a platform of faithfulness.

When you live authentically, you're easy to love. It's attractive. You become like a magnet. You attract favor and opportunity and people who can help you step up into God's best for your life.

It has been said that we should concern ourselves with the depth of our ministry and let God worry about the breadth. There is so much truth to that statement. If you steep your life in authenticity, credibility, and consistency, it is God who brings the increase.

One of my best friends has been a part of my life for more than thirty years. He is a successful businessman who has weathered the ups and downs of economic times and both the thriving joy and the devastating loss that have come with ownership. Yet even through the toughest of times, it was his credibility and faithfulness that caused other people to stand with him and continue to invest in his dreams. Without such qualities in his character, his business would have surely failed.

Let's live authentically. Let's be genuine. Honest and faithful in our marriages, friendships, and business partnerships. It was because Timothy was a true son—a man of credibility and authenticity—that Paul poured himself into and invested in him. Your words will have more weight, your opportunities will go further, and your dreams will have a sturdy foundation to be built upon when faithfulness is your platform.

Every week I have the opportunity to stand on the platform at Hillsong Church. But I have a greater platform. Forty-four years of active ministry, forty years of faithful marriage to the wife of my youth, and thirty-three years pastoring the same church give me a platform of credibility and faithfulness that will get me further than any natural platform

I construct. I've often been asked the question "How long does it take you to prepare a message?" and my answer is always "Sixty-three years" (or whatever age I am at the time).

I recently attended the funeral of a dear friend. He was seventy-four years old when he died. At the service to celebrate his life, his wife of fifty-plus years, his children, and their spouses and countless grandchildren dotted the stage, facing hundreds of people in attendance to pay respects to their husband, father, granddad, and friend. It got me thinking: he didn't build that family in a day. He didn't meet all these people over the course of just one year or two. In that room were seventy-four years of building relationship: going to school plays, attending sports matches, disciplining and encouraging young people, being a shoulder to lean on and a hand to hold. To some people in that room, he represented a friendly neighbor; to others, he was a constant friend, a mentor, a teacher. He built relationships throughout his life, and it was so obvious on that day. Faithfulness builds, and faithfulness stays.

Similarly, a new friend of mine, Bob Goff, author of *Love Does,* puts his phone number in the back of his books. When asked why, he simply replies, "The most important people in my life have always been the ones who are most available." It's a simple and profound truth and one that has led to many interesting conversations, meetings, and unexpected encounters, I'm sure! Authenticity, credibility, and consistency—simply being available when you are needed—don't go unnoticed.

Indeed, our consistency of vision, track record of faithfulness, and authentic faith in Christ will build a platform for the more that is in our hearts. If you want to make a difference and leave a legacy, you've got to live a life of authenticity, credibility, and consistency that inspires others to do the same.

9

The Walk and
the War

How weird are crop circles—those huge, unexplained, perfectly symmetrical circles in the middle of vast fields. Taking into account mysterious lights, unsolved mysteries, science fiction, and movies such as *ET,* humans have long been intrigued by the possibility of alternate life forms. Hundreds of movies, fables, and research papers have documented what people have "seen" in the heavenlies, often explained logically by some third-party skeptic or doubting scientist.

But it was one well-regarded American businessman, mathematician, and astronomer who captured the world's attention when his research showed up on the front page of the *New York Times* in August 1907 with the headline "Mars Inhabited."* Professor Percival Lowell had identified canals on the Red Planet that were thousands of miles long and far too straight (he said) to be a natural phenomenon. From his observatory in Flagstaff, Arizona, he studied these canals in great detail and

---

* David W. Dunlap, "Life on Mars? You Read It Here First," *New York Times,* October 1, 2015, www.nytimes.com/2015/09/30/insider/life-on-mars-you-read-it-here-first.html?_r=1.

concluded they must be signs of supernatural life. Aliens living and working together on the faraway planet. Martians!

The public was fascinated by his research, but the scientific community was skeptical. Other scientists tried to see what he was seeing, and the US government even built a larger and more powerful telescope to further the investigation. Years later, not only was Lowell's theory discredited, but it was widely believed that a glitch in his telescope had caused him to see the reflection of the red veins in his own eyes, misinterpreting what he saw as canals on the surface of Mars! What he thought was a supernatural phenomenon was actually a natural one. How embarrassing!

Both spiritual and natural roadblocks are givens when pursuing lives of more. Forging new ground will undoubtedly uncover new battles, and it's crucial that we properly identify the type of battle we're facing. It will influence how we confront the challenges, how we deal with the fallout, and how we walk in consistency in our daily lives, both on the good days and the bad days—and that's what really matters!

What about you? Have you come up against spiritual roadblocks that have manifested themselves in natural ways? Perhaps you are feeling a lag in your spiritual growth, leaving you unmotivated in the natural to do such things as worship, read your Bible, and attend church. Often something believed to be a spiritual problem is simply a natural one. On the other hand, maybe you are facing a natural problem that actually has a spiritual solution. Or maybe you are experiencing natural resistance to the spiritual possibilities in your life. Let me explain.

At the time we were pioneering Hillsong Church, our family car was a Datsun 180b. It was a faded red coupe with a bubbling black vinyl roof. Unfortunately, our little car looked as if it had been through both world wars. Not only that but it had a serious rust problem, which led to our only form of transportation being deemed unsafe and not roadworthy by the local authorities. In those days, we struggled to find the money for fuel each week, let alone the ability to afford having the rust cut out, a new paint job, and the repairs needed to keep our early 1970s car on the road. We needed the car not only to get our two toddlers and ourselves to church but also to pick up the plethora of people we brought each week to services. Momentum was stalled when the car was sidelined.

Did you know that your spiritual life could resemble my little roadster? Too many people pray for a spiritual answer to their natural problem. It's as though they are laying hands on the roof of their old, beat-up car, even though it is unlikely to make any difference if they are not putting fuel in the tank. Just saying!

Don't misunderstand what I'm saying. Prayer for miracles (supernatural breakthrough) to natural problems (sickness and disease) is so important, and God cares deeply about those things. And just as much as God cares about our natural problems, He cares about our spiritual worries as well. But too many of us can have stalled momentum (like that of the little car) on our life journeys. While searching for spiritual breakthrough, we can fail to progress instead of taking necessary and sometimes painful steps in the natural to bring change. God has put everything in place to deliver us and bring answers to every area of our lives, but we must first commit to remaining steadfast in our resolve that nothing can stand in the way of the lives God intended for us.

The road to discovering all that God has for you is paved with natural habits and devotion that can bring about the spiritual solution you are looking for. In fact, the natural and spiritual lives flow together perfectly if you allow them.

Similarly, the resistance we sometimes feel in our everyday lives can affect our spiritual lives in a negative way. Friend, you have God on your side, and He has made a way for you in both the natural and the supernatural. Unfortunately, so many people just don't want to do the hard work of transformation.

Creator and Corruptor

Humankind lasted exactly two chapters and five verses without sin. Yes, it was only a couple of chapters!

The early Genesis account records how God knit together the earth. He formed the oceans and spoke into existence both the night and the day. And four verses in, the Bible tells us that the Lord saw that it was good. It's repeated several times that the Lord's creation was very good. Imagine that—calling what's currently our creaking, shuddering, impoverished, and tainted world "good"!

But it wasn't always a creaking, shuddering, impoverished, and tainted earth. You see, our God is a creator. He fashioned a perfect world, devoid of sin and mistake, pain and wrongdoing. Before the fall of man, in the space of two and a bit chapters, He established absolutes, laws, companionship, marriage, work, rest, creativity, multiplication, a sense of purpose, and choice for His people.

All these natural qualities are God's own handiwork, so—clearly—not everything natural is a result of sin's destructive consequence. And regardless of what you may have been taught up to this point, the Enemy (Satan) could not destroy what God has created. But he could *corrupt* it.

And corrupt he did.

Through the temptation of Adam and Eve, sin entered the world and gave way to the powers of spiritual darkness on the earth. The things that God created for good could now be twisted and misused, abused and led astray. Let me elaborate.

God created food. Most of us love food, and it was created to sustain and nurture our bodies. But when we corrupt the love of food, it can become gluttony. In the same way, having a distorted body image can cause both obesity and eating disorders—epidemics in today's society. This is a very real example of a good gift from God becoming aberrant under the weight of pressure from the Enemy.

Also, God created sex. I, for one, am glad He did! Within the sacred commitment of a healthy marriage, sex is the design of a creative and kind God. Not only for procreation but also for enjoyment and intimacy, sex is a gift. But all around us, it is easy to see the outcome of corrupted sex. Distorted, sex can become lustful, and dark spiritual forces can turn it into a perverse action, causing destructive and devastating consequences.

It can be easy when looking at life like this to allow ourselves to think that everything is bad. One flick of the remote can land us watching world news that will consistently barrage us with stories of despair and horror—people facing enormous physical challenges such as war, injury, and abuse. We all have stories to tell when it comes to battles we've faced in the natural realm: sickness of loved ones, difficult conversations with bosses, failed projects, and discouraging reports. It is easy to develop an attitude that says that life is too hard.

But we don't need to constantly fight the natural world. Instead, we need to live within the truth of His promises that He has overcome (see John 16:33). We need to look at challenges with spiritual eyes and natural wisdom and channel every circumstance for good. *This* is the pathway to abundant life.

Let me challenge you for a moment. Did you know that God has equipped you through the Holy Spirit and His Word to walk in absolute freedom? Do you think that sometimes we look for spiritual answers simply because we want God to do all the work? Too many people are praying to be delivered from their smoking addiction (or some other destructive dependency) when deliverance isn't even the answer; rather, what they need is an overcoming spirit! Maybe, just maybe, if they would recognize who they are in Christ, the strength they can access through His Word, and the power that is theirs through the Holy Spirit, they could develop the discipline and commitment they need to live as an overcomer. (Side note: Obviously, smoking in and of itself isn't going to send you to hell. But it *is* an addiction you can overcome.)

Do you understand what I mean? The solution may need natural steps. Sure, you need God's help on the journey, but don't mistake His miraculous power as a substitute for wisdom and work. I encourage you to make daily decisions that will enable you to conquer your negative habits and destructive behaviors.

Spiritual answers are wonderful. An unexplainable miracle or unexpected breakthrough, a supernatural healing or the windows of heaven opening with overflowing blessings—yes! How amazing that Christ can and does make all these things possible because of the victory He has won on our behalf! Let's thank God for every miraculous possibility He brings our way. But I find it intriguing to learn from Scripture that although there were various and multiple times God brought instant and dramatic deliverance to people, there were also other times in which issues or afflictions held people bound and so He instead gave them all the *tools* they needed to overcome.

Looking in the Bible, it's difficult to find any examples of God bringing instant deliverance to discipline issues such as smoking and addiction. Throughout Scripture, we see that God delivered His people from such things as plagues, pestilence, floods, sickness, disease, and demonic forces. These are things that are beyond human control and that only He has the power to change. But what about when things are within our own power to change? Are we too often expecting God to deliver us from something He's given us the power to overcome?

Remember, you have the strengthening power of the Holy Spirit residing within you. The Word of God, sharper than a two-edged sword, is available to you. You go by His name, and the authority you need is in the name of Jesus—a name that is higher than every conceivable power working against you. This means you are perfectly poised to rise up, stand strong, and live as more than a conqueror and overcomer in this fallen world. The same power that raised Christ from the dead now dwells in you, and it's His power that delivers and equips you to stand tall as an overcomer.

So I guess your big question may be "When does God bring deliverance to me, and when does He want me to rise up, stand firm, and take natural steps to overcome?" Good question.

I know that addicts often feel powerless to overcome their own addiction. Perhaps they have earnestly tried many times and many things to be free from that which binds them. This takes great courage and inner fortitude and should never be diminished. I know of many people who are convinced God has delivered them miraculously from addiction, and I certainly believe that He can do just that! But I also believe that we must be prepared to take up the challenge to live by His Word and equip ourselves with the spiritual armory for the battle.

Acknowledge that God has given you the tools to let go, have the courage to walk away, rise above, and change the way you think about your problem in order to move forward. As we discovered earlier in this chapter, the natural and spiritual were both created by God, and the partnership between our part and His part is a great study.

Baby Steps

I want you to notice a pattern in these words from the apostle Paul: "It is written, 'The first MAN, Adam, BECAME A LIVING SOUL.' The last Adam became a life-giving spirit. However, the spiritual is not first, but the natural; then the spiritual. The first man is from the earth, earthy; the second man is from heaven" (1 Corinthians 15:45–47, NASB).

Did you notice the pattern? *First* the natural and *then* the spiritual.

Did you know that what you put first in your life will undoubtedly determine your future? For example, 1 Timothy 3:5 tells us, "If anyone does not know how to manage his own family, how can he take care of God's church?" (NIVII). In other words, the fulfillment of my calling, and yours, begins in our homes—in our personal walk with Jesus, the daily decisions we make, and the disciplines we instill (in our natural lives) in order to follow God into the miraculous provision and abundance, blessing and favor, freedom and fulfillment He has purposed for us.

There are so many things clamoring for our attention on a daily basis—our jobs, kids, spouses, friends, hobbies. It is not the will of God that you would cast any of these aside for the sake of ministry or spiritual fulfillment. Instead, God bids us to get our natural lives in order and then watch our spiritual lives take healthy shape.

God said to Abraham, "Walk and live habitually before Me and be perfect (blameless, wholehearted, complete)" (Genesis 17:1, AMPC). Live *habitually*—I believe it is no coincidence that this word is used here. Our habits form our foundations, and our foundations are extremely important when it comes to walking and warring in both the natural and spiritual realms.

What does it mean to "war" in the spiritual realm? Well, the Bible clearly tells us that we are in a spiritual battle. In fact, Ephesians 6:10–20 talks about putting on the full armor of God: truth, peace, righteousness, faith, and salvation. Do your habits form within you the kind of foundations that allow you to both walk in the natural and war in the spirit? The kind of foundations that God can build upon?

I think the MVP of the NBA, the Heisman Trophy winner, the winners of the UEFA Champions League, and those athletes holding aloft the Rugby World Cup know exactly this notion. They comprehend that the big win wasn't when they were handed the trophy; the win was in the daily decision to practice, to get good grades in high school and play by the rules in college, to choose the healthiest option over and over rather than the number-five meal at the burger joint or the pizza at the party. It was the early-morning runs on rainy days when bed looked so inviting but discipline demanded something other than mediocrity.

Please don't feel condemned or discouraged at this point. I'm mostly preaching to myself in this chapter! I too need to continually commit to the daily disciplines of living an overcoming life, recognizing that God has so much more for me in the later years of my journey.

I truly believe that it was forty-four years of taking baby steps in the natural—committing my ways to the Lord, attending Bible college, living faithfully, being diligent with our finances, being honest in our relationships—that has allowed Bobbie and me the spiritual blessing and breakthrough that we experience today. The flourishing nature of our church, our home, and our private lives has so much more to do with the small steps we took to ensure our foundations were right than it does with any luck or providence that people may chalk it up to. I shudder to think where we might be without God's amazing grace. And it's grace, not striving, that forms and guides our baby steps along the way.

You've probably heard that old description "Too spiritually minded for any earthly good." I think an excessive number of Christians concern themselves with simply getting their spiritual lives in order, while dismissing the idea that their everyday steps have any lasting or eternal value. Friend, you begin to lack relevance and significance in the world about you if you fail to realize that your relationship to it is extremely important. Your daily devotional life, home life, thought life, relational life, work life, and private life are all of importance to God and to your witness as a follower of Jesus Christ.

Colossians 1:17 reads, "He is before all things, and in Him all things consist." *All* things consist. The big things *and* the little things.

The Walk and the War

Consider this wise description of our condition: "Though we *walk* in the flesh, we do not *war* according to the flesh. For the weapons of our warfare are not carnal but mighty in God for pulling down strongholds, casting down arguments and every high thing that exalts itself against the knowledge of God, bringing every thought into captivity to the obedience of Christ, and being ready to punish all disobedience when your obedience is fulfilled" (2 Corinthians 10:3–6).

Walking in the natural world and warring in the spiritual realm—this is our reality. The Bible says so. But just as we've already concluded, the natural and the spiritual are not opposing forces. They are not mutually exclusive to one another. When redeemed, they can go perfectly hand in hand.

So many of us are good at one and not the other. Many people are excellent when it comes to warring in the spirit. They are the first at the prayer meeting and the last to leave. Their ability to discern the needs of others and listen to the promptings of the Spirit often encourage and uplift. Yet their bills never get paid. Their lawns are not mowed and their cars are a mess. Their lack of attention to the everyday responsibilities of life can cause chaos.

Others are good at the walk but terrible at the war. They are disciplined and organized. Home and work are harmonious, and people see them as well put together, with all their ducks in a row. But come any sign of a spiritual battle, and they fall to pieces, although God says that's when we must "put on the whole armor of God . . . [to] be able to stand against the wiles of the devil. For we do not wrestle against flesh and blood, but against principalities, against powers, against the rulers of the darkness of this age, against spiritual hosts of wickedness in the heavenly places. Therefore take up the whole armor of God, that you may be able to withstand in the evil day, and having done all, to stand" (Ephesians 6:11–13).

What is it that you are wrestling with? How is your walk and how is your war? Which area of your life is lacking the balance you need to move forward in one area or another? What big spiritual answers are you looking for when the natural solutions are staring you in the face?

Take Your Everyday
and Ordinary Life

The natural and supernatural can work together beautifully. In the words of Paul to the Romans, "Here's what I want you to do, God helping you: Take your everyday, ordinary life—your sleeping, eating, going-to-work, and walking-around life—and place it before God as an offering. Embracing what God does for you is the best thing you can do for him" (Romans 12:1, MSG).

I know this raises questions. Allow me to address, one by one, some of the questions that I hear over and over again about this topic.

"How Can I Know the Mind of the Spirit?"

It's a question I've heard a time or ten in my tenure as a pastor. So many of us want to know what is in God's heart for our futures or what the Spirit is speaking, yet we fail to confront the muddle in our own mind. What I mean is that the spiritual question is "How can I know the mind of the Spirit?" but the natural solution is simply to clear your own head of double-mindedness, confusion, and doubt and step forward in faith! The writer of Romans 12:2 bids us, "Do not conform to the pattern of this world, but be transformed by the renewing of your mind. Then you will be able to test and approve what God's will is—his good, pleasing and perfect will" (NIV11).

You must commit to the continual process of renewing your mind before you can know the mind of the Spirit. If your head is filled with negativity and self-doubt, if you are constantly struggling with anxiety and restless behavior, then that is what you must first address. Along with searching for spiritual answers, seek out help. Speak to someone trustworthy and work at lessening the "noise" and changing the pattern of behavior that has potentially kept you from hearing from God.

"How Do I Fulfill My God-Given Potential?"

A number of years ago, two young friends were catching a morning wave in the city of Newcastle, located a two-hour drive north of Sydney. Newcastle is a city of natural beauty, with endless beaches and great surf, but it has historically been better known for its industry than for academia. The two young surfers in the water that day were Lee Burns and Scott ("Sanga") Samways. Lee told Sanga that he had been thinking a lot about moving to Sydney to attend Hillsong College. Little did he know that Sanga also had been researching schools that would prepare him for full-time ministry. In that moment, Lee's longtime friend and surfing buddy replied enthusiastically that he too would enroll at Hillsong College—a choice that neither of them knew at the time would indelibly affect their entire lives.

Arriving at Hillsong Church, these two wide-eyed men made quite an impression on their classmates with their long, flowing hair and relaxed surfer demeanors. But both came hungry to learn and threw themselves into college life and greater involvement in church with all the enthusiasm of two young guns with a dream. It wasn't long before they were both occupying significant leadership roles in the youth ministry, while Lee also worked part time during his college days, packing boxes and fulfilling orders in the storeroom of Hillsong Music. Later, I learned that the "background music" he was famous for playing over the speakers at work was not music at all. He would almost always be listening to teaching and preaching from notable ministries around the world, devouring the Word of God with an appetite that has never really diminished.

Today God has led Sanga, his beautiful Bulgarian wife (whom he met at Hillsong College), and their children back to Newcastle as the campus pastors of one of our rapidly growing Hillsong locations. He is undoubtedly one of our best preachers, his communication style unique and unrivaled. And Lee is the executive vice president of Hillsong College, overseeing a significant staff and a student body of more than two thousand young people from more than sixty countries. And although Lee has a wonderful, growing family and carries large responsibilities in a demanding role, he is well on his way to acquiring a PhD in theology, devoting many hours a week above all his other responsibilities to equip himself to fulfill his potential. It's been quite a journey from the surf of a working-class town to the global opportunities and influence he is enjoying today.

I am always impressed by people like Lee who take it upon themselves to further their studies simply as a habit of discipline or obedience. No one asked them to; they just recognized that their calling could require more of them than they possessed at the time. Lee knew that to fulfill all that God was asking of him, he needed to take practical, natural steps in order to boost his understanding of the supernatural.

Lee reminds me of another young ministry leader, to whom Paul said, "Work hard so you can present yourself to God and receive his approval. Be a good worker, one who does not need to be ashamed and who correctly explains the word of truth" (2 Timothy 2:15, NLT). Now, don't misconstrue the intent of that verse. It does not give license for striving and is not saying that in order to be approved by God, you are to check off a list of requirements. Instead, take it as a challenge. Are you feeling a stall in your momentum toward that which God has called you to? Perhaps there are practical steps you can take to break through the barrier holding you back.

"How Do I Experience the 'Open Window' Blessings of Heaven?"

The "open window" refers to the book of Malachi, where God makes a promise to His people, saying, "Test me in this and see if I will not throw open the floodgates of heaven and pour out so much blessing that there will not be room enough to store it" (3:10, NIVII).

More often than you would expect, this question is followed by a statement such as "I tithe 10 percent every weekend!" My response might seem probing, but without fail I would inquire, "Do you use wisdom with your finances? Are you making good everyday decisions and getting the right kind of advice needed to plan appropriately for your future?"

God's financial blessings are just as much about diligence in the natural realm as obedience in the spiritual realm.

"Why Is the Devil Attacking My Family?"

The Enemy knows how to hurt us, and many times there are no explanations for his choice of attack other than he's trying to knock us off course. But the Word of God gives us wisdom in this area also: "Husbands, live with your wives in an understanding way, showing honor to the woman as the weaker vessel, since they are heirs with you of the grace of life, so that your prayers may not be hindered" (1 Peter 3:7, ESV). Are you treating your wife (your husband, your family) with honor? Do you love them like Christ loved the church? Or do you need to repent of the way you have spoken to or acted toward those you love? The Bible is clear that our spiritual lives can suffer hindrance if this natural area is not in order.

"Why Isn't Our Church Seeing Revival?"

Over many years, I've watched churches the world over pray for increase. They might start every year with a twenty-one-day fast or hold daily prayer meetings. They may even organize prayer walks and point to the north, south, east, and west while binding demons. They may constantly petition God for revival but never seem to get their breakthrough. This is not a commentary on any of those practices, and their devotion and desperation are commendable. But perhaps they've failed to address some basics, such as creating a genuine sense of "Welcome home!" or foundational elements that would not only draw people in but also meet some of their practical needs. For example, maybe their services never start on time and their finishing time is forever unknown. Or perhaps children are allowed to run out of control and distract those around them from receiving the Word. Or perhaps the people in church leadership are notoriously poor stewards of finance. Each of these things can be a natural barrier to spiritual answers.

Have you stopped to think about the natural barriers to your spiritual immobility?

Early in 2017, I proudly walked through the new Epicentre facility on our Hills Campus property. Years of sacrificial giving had seen this new building come to life. I was thrilled to see the new facilities for children and youth and astounded at the care and detail that had gone into the planning to accommodate families with additional needs, including rooms specially designed so that young people with autism could go to church and not be overwhelmed. For years we prayed that our church would have a greater reach into our community and would find ways to be relevant and engaging to families who were met with additional challenges. But we didn't *just* pray; we also researched and planned and sacrificially gave for a long time before being positioned to build. We took natural steps to ensure that our prayers would be answered, and I believe it was both our natural walk and our spiritual war that enabled this supernatural miracle.

Impossible Possibilities

Perhaps you've been reading this chapter so far and thinking, *Sure, Brian, but you don't know the things I am coming up against. My family is a mess. The resistance we are experiencing in our work and ministry is extreme, not to mention the health challenges and financial strain.*

I do understand. Life can be unpredictable and downright discouraging. But have faith, my friend. Stories of impossible possibilities fill the Bible. To God, all things are possible; therefore, *with Him* nothing is impossible. Just to believe in Him means you believe in impossible possibilities, which opens you up to the realm of miracles. A miracle is an impossible possibility. The will of God for our lives and the walk of faith are impossible possibilities. Grace is an impossible possibility. Salvation encompasses the unrighteous made righteous—that in itself is an impossible possibility. Serving God is full of impossible possibilities, but there is always resistance, and often the greatest resistance is not external but internal.

Many years ago, we had a life-changing experience when Bobbie, Laura (our daughter), and I traveled to Uganda. We were there to see the work of Compassion International for the first time and traveled to an area called Kasese, where our church sponsors thousands of Ugandan children to make a way for them to receive an education, health care, clothing, and ongoing counsel for family well-being. The roads were poor and the trip slow going.

On our way back, we got to a long stretch of road that was leading toward a hill. I could see something in the distance rolling down the hill. It was a minibus with objects flying out of it. The brakes had failed and this bus was hurtling out of control, and to my dismay it turned out that the "objects" were people. We were the first to get to the accident scene. Bodies were spread out all over the place. Some people were screaming and yelling; others were quietly moaning or just silent; some appeared to be dying. We didn't know what to do, and while our Hillsong London pastors walked around doing what they could, I simply walked around praying for people. It was a horrific sight to behold.

A paramedic friend once told me that when you get to an accident, it's not the screamers you go to first; it's the ones who are making no noise. Those who are screaming are usually suffering external injuries, but the ones who are quiet often have internal injuries, which are more devastating and life threatening than external problems. I have never forgotten that, because I believe it is also true in life and ministry.

Doubt, insecurity, procrastination, fear—these are internal issues. Possibility has so much resistance, but the most powerful opposition you will face is internal. What is going on inside you can be far more devastating than what is going on outside, yet often what you see on the outside is a reflection of what is going on inside. Your heart can become injured from heartbreak and betrayal. The lens through which you view life can be tainted by the bad things that happen to you, and it is easy to put a wall up to protect your heart. There is wisdom in protecting your heart from harmful things, but insulating your heart from God or drawing back from His leading could send you into a spiral of both natural and spiritual tribulation.

Win the Daily Battle

The life of the prophet Daniel inspires me. In Daniel 6:3, he is described as having an "excellent spirit." Despite confronting serious resistance for so much of his life, he kept winning victories on the inside. I believe that what was on the inside of him was the very thing that provided a way forward and a pathway for his future.

Bound to a foreign land, language, and culture against his will, with nothing familiar and no one to lean on, Daniel kept rising to the top. He had divine favor with three different kings: Nebuchadnezzar, Darius, and Cyrus. And even when his community resented him for rising in status, they could not fault him, because he was faithful. They contrived to use his faithfulness to God against him because that's all they could do. So they entrapped him, leading to one of the most shared stories in the Bible about his supernatural deliverance from a pack of hungry lions (see Daniel 6).

Natural resistance routinely came up against Daniel, but the Bible tells us that he had internal strength: "This Daniel became distinguished above all the other high officials and satraps, because an excellent spirit was in him. And the king planned to set him over the whole kingdom" (verse 3, ESV). He walked in blessing and prosperity because he was healthy on the inside.

So often when you face persecution, it is not about you but about the God you serve. The antichrist spirit that is so prevalent will try to bring you down. But do as Daniel did: distinguish yourself. Allow your heart posture to be one of overcoming, determined to win the daily battles in the natural realm that will lead to your spiritual favor. As He did with Daniel, God will deliver you and favor you despite the external resistance because what is inside you is greater than what happens to you.

Allow God to continue to work internally on your heart and spirit, and allow Him to lead you and have His way. Let Him break down the resistance of your heart that undermines His power in you. Live your life in charge of your spirit and heart, and see God cause you to rise above every circumstance and challenge you face.

And commit to winning the daily battles. The mediocre ones. The casual ones. The *habitual* ones.

Continue to grow in both your walk *and* your war. Build a foundation for spiritual success through the daily natural choices to love, forgive, and let go. Be a champion of your marriage; be an encourager of your children.

Be someone's courage, hope, and compassion, and be constantly filled with faith for each new day. Then watch as God takes your natural ability and turns it into unending spiritual possibility.

10

Troubling the Troubler

The red and blue lights started flashing, and that's when I knew I was in trouble. It had been just another day, waiting after school with my older brother, Graeme, at the church where my parents were pastors. Often our wait was long, and finding ways to break the monotony was a daily occurrence, meaning mischief was never far away.

We were only one block from the church office, where I knew my mum and dad would be working away, oblivious to the mayhem my brother and I were causing. We hadn't meant any harm, but the little motorbike had just been sitting there, begging to be taken for a spin. I knew that the owner, a Bible college student, was in class and unlikely to need his bike for several more hours, so what harm could come of a little joyride? Or so I thought. We were bored and the temptation was far too great for a pair of adolescent siblings.

I panicked when I spotted the policeman and tried to stop the motorbike by dragging my feet on the ground. My conspicuous act caught his attention. Sure enough, he pointed to the side of the road, beckoning me to pull over, and I knew I was in trouble.

I trembled when the officer asked to see my license. Obviously I didn't have one, as I was only thirteen. My fear of punishment was far greater than my need for adventure, and the punishment that I received from my father was enough to keep me on the straight and narrow for a long time to come. So I'd love to say that was the last bit of trouble I ever got into, but we all know that isn't the truth.

My teenage years and college days were marked by lighthearted mischief, and my older years have often found me bringing somewhat humorous misfortune to my own life. I've walked into a glass door with a broken shoulder, slipped down the stairs with my socks on, and unknowingly shaved a lawnmower-type strip into my own hair just before one of our major conferences (after forgetting to put the comb on the end of my clippers). I've locked my notes in a random broom cupboard immediately before I preached on a Sunday morning. And I've connected my head with the sharp edge of a door just minutes before taking the platform in Baton Rouge, Louisiana, where I was about to speak at a pastors' conference, streamed live on the Daystar Television Network (which I painfully proceeded to do with an egg-like bump and a bloodied cut right in the middle of my forehead).

I can laugh at most of these troublesome circumstances now, but have you noticed that trouble seems to follow some people? However, I don't believe that we, as followers of Christ, are called to be on only the receiving end of trouble.

The Troubler or the Troublee?

The devil, in his efforts to discourage us, loves to bring trouble our way. Family, financial, and health crises seem to befall each of us at certain times of life, often crushing our spirits and stopping us in our tracks.

Grief, pain, loss, and heartache are catalysts for other serious issues, such as anxiety and depression.

I can imagine you are tired of picking up books that refer to the ugly, desperate, disillusioning circumstances you face as "light and momentary" (2 Corinthians 4:17, NIVII). And as much as I can surely understand this verse, I am also no stranger to the issues of life that feel anything *but* light and momentary. Yet the verse that precedes it continually grabs me, causes me to sit up and take notice, and puts fight back in my spirit. "We do not lose heart. Though outwardly we are wasting away, yet inwardly we are being renewed day by day" (verse 16, NIVII).

Inward renewal, internal fortification, a momentum that propels you forward—this is my hope for you. I pray that you would discover a life that moves forward rather than one that is on retreat—that you would live a life that actually troubles the power of darkness rather than succumbs to it. I have no doubt you can.

In Acts 16, we observe the journey of Paul, Timothy, and Silas as they ministered throughout the nations, including a momentous stop in Philippi of Macedonia. "Now it happened, as we went to prayer, that a certain slave girl possessed with a spirit of divination met us, who brought her masters much profit by fortune-telling. This girl followed Paul and us, and cried out, saying, 'These men are the servants of the Most High God, who proclaim to us the way of salvation'" (verses 16–17). Can you imagine the annoyance for Paul and Barnabas? The spirits within this girl were driving her to behave like a stalker by pursuing them every day and everywhere. Not content to simply follow them, she continually interrupted their ministry with her incessant yelling for many days. The inference is that because she was possessed by an evil spirit, her tone was mocking and her goal was to sidetrack and distract Paul and Barnabas and their followers from the true message they came to speak. No wonder Paul was "greatly annoyed" (verse 18)!

I've seen my fair share of hecklers. I've watched people come into church meetings drunk, unbalanced, or simply with agendas to draw attention away from the Word of God. They're filled with a spirit of ill intent and hell-bent on causing trouble. I don't blame Paul for his annoyance! He had just about enough, and one day he whipped around and said to the spirit within the slave girl, "I command you in the name of Jesus Christ to come out of her" (verse 18). Here's what happened:

> He came out that very hour. But when her masters saw that their hope of profit was gone, they seized Paul and Silas and dragged them into the marketplace to the authorities.
>
> And they brought them to the magistrates, and said, "These men, being Jews, exceedingly *trouble* our city." (verses 18–20)

From Philippi, they moved on to Thessalonica, where people rumored in the streets that the same men who had turned the world upside down were now right there on their turf, causing chaos in their very own backyard. Next on the journey for these itinerant apostles was Corinth, where there was fury about Paul teaching new believers to worship. From there, they journeyed to Ephesus, sparking a major revolt amongst silversmiths who were profiteering from their mass-produced statuettes of the goddess Diana. You see, the potential impact of these men on their dubious enterprise left them fearful and furious as these Jesus followers converted many away from pagan gods.

Trouble, trouble, trouble. As they preached Christ with power, the disciples upset people's sense of familiarity. In particular, the Pharisees, government officials, religious leaders, and unreceptive unbelievers were thoroughly threatened by the changes they saw in people who they perceived were robbing them of control, territory, conformity, and containment. Without the evil spirit within her, the slave girl's masters made no money—so they lost control!

The good news continued to be spread, reaching Macedonia, Greece, and Turkey and causing religious leaders, in particular, to be threatened by an overwhelming fear that they were losing ground. People began to get free from their religious confines, and leaders began to lose conformity. How dare Paul worship outside the religious box in which everyone was expected to conform! How dare he make Jesus Christ the object of worship! As the crowds began to discover the Son of God, that discovery turned their lives and cities upside down. In fact, the apostle and his traveling companions were turning the whole world upside down. In essence, they "troubled the troubler," and that's exactly what Jesus did.

Upside-Down Kingdom

High above the Sea of Galilee, Jesus spoke words of truth that would forever shape history. He turned religion on its head, opened the eyes of unbelievers, and gave new meaning to old ideals. He shattered the preconceptions of His followers and caused them to question all they once knew of religion as He defied old doctrine by saying such things as "You have heard that it was said, 'Eye for eye and tooth for tooth.' But I tell you not to resist an evil person. If someone slaps you on your right cheek, turn to him the other also" (Matthew 5:38–39, BSB) or "Love your enemies, bless those who curse you" (verse 44). Jesus confounded the wisdom of the world.

As a believer, you too can turn your world upside down by defying the work of the Enemy and leading in a countercultural way. I love that our belief in the "now and not yet" of the kingdom of God means that love triumphs over hate, peace is more prevalent than fear, hope is available for the hopeless, and beauty comes from ashes. I love when our churches are moving forward despite the media headlines of "dying religion." I love when our young people are promoting kindness and compassion while the Enemy bombards a generation with violence and hate.

It would be easier if we could simply say that as Christians we aren't going to experience any trouble. But that wouldn't be true. Jesus Himself experienced the death of friends, the fear of pain, and the hurt of rejection.

In Matthew 14, we read how Jesus mourned the beheading of His beloved cousin John the Baptist. Scripture tells us that He sought out a desolate place to be alone in His grief and unwillingly happened upon a crowd looking to be ministered to. It was in this moment that Christ exemplified a response that not only messed with the devil but also furthered the kingdom. He healed people. He prayed. He ministered. He spoke the word of truth and watched the kingdom of God advance on that hill.

Yes, there must be time to acknowledge our trouble—time to grieve and time to seek wisdom. But there must also be an internal steadiness that outweighs the loss, a fight inside you that precedes the pain, a spirit that says, "I'm going to trouble the troubler and make him pay for the pain he's caused me." Yes, seek the desolate place, but don't set up camp there. You can visit, and that's okay, beneficial even, but don't live there. Watch the Lord fulfill His promise that day by day by day, He'll bring renewal on the inside. Hold fast to the knowledge that, yes, the kingdom is coming but it has also already come and we must live as though it already has. The world we live in is a fallen one, but it is also being made new every day. Bad things happen, trouble keeps on coming, but we must live as if the kingdom does too.

Several times I've visited Gethsemane. On a recent visit I stood by a cave in close view of the Old City walls, and there I meditated on Jesus's loneliness, desperation, and desolation in that garden moment. But you and I know He is no longer there. He didn't linger or set up camp. It was a pause, a moment, a desperate prayer He made in that garden that moved Him forward to embrace all that was ahead.

Promised Territory

There is no doubt about it: with territory come enemies. In 2002, Hillsong first opened our convention center (to this day, our largest gathering place). It was an amazing day that shouted a story about years of faithfulness, both from our generous congregation and the Lord. Blessing and breakthrough marked the moment when we opened the doors to our new auditorium and put a stake in the ground for a church that had vision to grow beyond its borders. The prime minister of Australia was our honored guest. Indeed, leaders came from all over the country, drawing attention to this emerging company of passionate believers in the northwestern suburbs of Sydney.

That's when the trouble started.

Years before, I sat down to write about the church I envisioned. A line I wrote became painstakingly true as we put a literal stake in the ground. It said, "The church that I see is so large in size that the city and nation cannot ignore it." And ignore it they did not. To put it into context, it was as though a church that already was known among believers through all continents of the earth was not really known at all by secular Australia. What followed were ten years of intense scrutiny and media coverage (mostly negative) from almost every media outlet you can imagine. The news was trying to fathom how in a climate where church attendance is supposed to be waning and Christianity is considered mainly irrelevant, a church could possibly be filled with both the young and the old, pulsating with life, and often packed to overflowing. It was a case of people criticizing what they couldn't or didn't want to understand, and—I believe—a spiritual attack aimed to discourage, dishearten, and disrupt a genuine move of the Holy Spirit.

I strongly believe there is something about church buildings that the devil hates. The permanence of believers putting real stakes in the ground in a city and nation irks the Enemy. For every attempt that was made to discredit us, all these years on we have many more buildings in Australia, worship songs reaching farther than ever before, a thriving Bible college, a global television channel, and thousands of people gathering in major cities across Europe, Africa, and North and South America. Most important of all, streams of people every week are coming to faith in Jesus Christ, and more than ever is being done to help the poor and the broken in the cities around the world where Hillsong Church gathers, as well as far-flung places such as Aleppo, Syria; Mumbai, India; and Gugulethu, South Africa. It's an ongoing and increasing testimony to the faithfulness of God and the resilience of His church. But there is nothing like progress to bring about opposition. Just ask Joshua.

Be Strong and Courageous

Nothing about the promise mentioned trouble or enemies. I can only imagine Joshua's chest puffing up a little as the God of the universe bestowed on him the ancient promise of Moses for new territory and expansive hope:

> I promise you what I promised Moses: "Wherever you set foot, you will be on land I have given you—from the Negev wilderness in the south to the Lebanon mountains in the north, from the Euphrates River in the east to the Mediterranean Sea in the west, including all the land of the Hittites." No one will be able to stand against you as long as you live. For I will be with you as I was with Moses. I will not fail you or abandon you. (Joshua 1:3–5, NLT)

Nope, there is nothing recorded there about trouble. But read carefully as the promise continues:

> Be strong and courageous, for you are the one who will lead these people to possess all the land I swore to their ancestors I would give them. Be strong and very courageous. Be careful to obey all the instructions Moses gave you. Do not deviate from them, turning either to the right or to the left. Then you will be successful in everything you do. Study this Book of Instruction continually. Meditate on it day and night so you will be sure to obey everything written in it. Only then will you prosper and succeed

in all you do. This is my command—be strong and courageous!
Do not be afraid or discouraged. For the LORD your God is with
you wherever you go. (verses 6–9, NLT)

Wait a minute—still nothing. Sounds pretty spectacular to me. I
know a few businesspeople and pastors (myself included) who wouldn't
mind some extra territory and promise of success. If everywhere he set his
foot was going to be his, why would Joshua need to be courageous? But
look closely. What does God say three times to Joshua? "Be strong and
courageous." I wonder if he ever stopped to wonder why.

You see, the passage never mentioned the thirty-one enemy kings he
would face *before* the promise was fulfilled (see Joshua 12). It never ac-
knowledged the endless battles, troubles, and rulers who would rise up
against Joshua and his people as they moved into the territory that God
had promised.

Don't be surprised, dear reader, when the Enemy rises up against you
just as you are pursuing your promise. Don't ever be shocked at the battles you face and the heartache that comes as you fight for new territory.
When you are gaining territory, the devil is *losing* it! As you serve Jesus,
it is His will that you would move forward into a life of exceeding abundance and promise, but it will not come without opposition. Just as He
did for Joshua, God wants to take your life forward, and just as it was for
Joshua, there will be kings to defeat.

Don't be discouraged, dear pastor, when your church is prospering
internally, when you are seeing salvation and growth and momentum,
and you begin to experience trouble financially. The tactics of the Enemy
are in direct proportion to your advancement; as your church is being

blessed, lives are being saved, and people are being impacted, the devil is going to do all he can to halt your progress. As God is doing the supernatural in your midst, with healings and blessings, provision and miracles, cynical hearts might begin to try to undermine credibility. Perhaps you've heard it said that the taller the tree, the more the wind blows. But the Word of God clearly tells us not to be afraid of taking ground. We need to understand that although there is opposition, God has called us to stand firm, to win and not lose. The Great Commission is all about advancing the kingdom of God and showing people salvation, and as you advance the will of God, you are also troubling the troubler!

The Bible tells us in Matthew 16:18 that the gates of hell will not prevail. I don't know about you, but I've never been attacked by a gate. Gates don't attack—they defend. And even the gates of hell can't hold back what God is doing!

Isaiah 59:19 says this:

When the enemy comes in like a flood,
The Spirit of the LORD will lift up a standard against him.

It's easy to think of the Enemy coming *against* us like a flood of trouble, but I have heard it said that changing the comma placement in the sentence should engender much more encouragement than fear. And that's why I like to remind my congregation, "When the enemy shall come in [pause], *like a flood* the Spirit of the Lord will lift up a standard against him and put him to flight."

Our God always prevails. I pray that you would continue to see the purposes of God moving you forward and that as you take new territory, your expectation is indeed that God will be your very present help in times of trouble. Don't step back—be strong and courageous and take new land. Look up and out and see the promises the Lord has given you.

Don't Be Silent

Silence is where the strongholds start. I truly believe that the culture we live in would have the church be silent—that the world says church should be contained in historic buildings with quiet organs and dying numbers. But I believe that troubling the troubler is all about increasing the volume and mounting the influence.

It was soon after the fortune-telling girl was silenced in Philippi that influential people were sufficiently troubled by the spread of the gospel message and the dynamic impact in the lives of everyday people that they decided enough was enough, marching Paul and Silas off to prison. This story stirs my spirit because it was their worship that set them free. The Bible says it was "at midnight" when the two men began to sing (see Acts 16:25). They found not only strength in their song but also joy in their day of trouble. In the same way, I believe that our worship breaks the silence, opens prison doors for others, and sets captives free.

The devil would love to hold you bound and control you. He would love to control your life, your finances, and your relationships and keep you from pressing onward and upward to the more that God has for you. He wants you to be tied up with the fear of disappointment, the shame of guilt, and the snare of sin. It's amazing how we can so often buy into his plan of control when we try to control our own problems by worrying or by looking only for natural solutions. But it is when we give over control of our lives and our troubles to Christ that we deny the Enemy territory, and freedom comes rushing in.

King David danced about wildly. The psalms recorded his worship, and even when his wife tried to box him in with her containing attitudes, David danced all the more.

I never want to box people in with any smallness that might be in my own spirit. My whole ministry is about equipping and empowering people to be all that God has called them to be. I long for that for you also. Don't contain people; don't make them small by thinking small. And in the same way, don't allow others to make you feel that way. Allow worship, partnership, and prayer to transform your thinking. Live loudly in a way that gives the Enemy no strongholds in your life. The religious leaders in Corinth were angered as Paul taught people to worship "contrary to the law" (Acts 18:13). But if Jesus is the source, there is no condemnation and containment in Christ. Instead, our worship must be marked by freedom—a choice to honor God with our lips and our lives.

I cannot encourage you enough to deny the Enemy his pleasure. Live with a sense of vision, attach it to a kingdom cause, and make your life a fortress of resilience, advancement, and blessing. To keep the devil from having any advantage, surround yourself with good people; understand the power of community to crowd out the plans of the Enemy.

You can overcome the things that oppose you—temptation, sin, fear, discouragement, depression, worry, hopelessness, addiction, anger, quitting, deception, weariness, burnout, stress, distress, poor choices, lack of wisdom, dependencies, insecurity, lack of confidence, sickness, pain, betrayal, heartbreak, backsliding, confusion—by living a life that defies the devil. We can be free in the face of any of these circumstances if we are marked by the fruit of the Spirit: love, joy, peace, patience, kindness, goodness, faithfulness, gentleness, and self-control. In the face of injustice, we can turn the other cheek. In the face of sickness, we can proclaim eternal healing. In the face of natural lack, we can proclaim spiritual abundance. We can bring trouble to the Enemy's plans where he intended to bring trouble to us.

Now is the time. Sow the Word of God in your heart and determine to live in pursuit of all God's promises—His *abundant* promises. Today is the day to rise up, stand up, be bold, be courageous, and be loud to trouble the troubler and enter into the exceedingly-above-all-you-can-ask-or-imagine promises of God.

11

Uncommon Grace and Unusual Miracles

I believe in miracles. The unexplainable kind. The big kind. The small kind. The everyday kind. The unusual kind. I've experienced miracles—been the recipient of them and the asker for them. No matter what time of year it is or what country in the world you are in, if you walk into a Hillsong Church service on any given weekend, you will most likely hear praise reports. We are a church that celebrates the good news. Prior to praying for people's needs (which we also do during every service), we lift up praise to God for the good testimony happening in the lives of people in our community. We thank Him for the big miracles and the small ones. We celebrate wins and even (if only just for a moment) applaud the answered prayer.

I've seen families receive anonymous blessings, individuals receive unexplainable healing, doctors be astounded at unusual breakthrough, businesspeople receive uncommon success, and people saved, restored, and brought back to relationship with Jesus in the most extraordinary ways.

Similarly, I've seen people battle through unanswered prayers and experience the heartache of situations that didn't turn out as they had petitioned. I've watched parents who prayed and still gave birth to babies they will never hold alive. I've watched good men and women take to their knees at enormous loss heaped on top of loss. I've watched death come in unexpected ways, and I've watched it come slowly despite the faithful prayers of many. I wish I could say that every one of my prayers has resulted in miracles, but of course that would not be true; there have been significant disappointments too. Yet I've watched people emerge from both miracles and disappointment with a confident declaration that they will forever believe in a God who does the extraordinary. Many times I've encouraged people never to lower their theology down to the level of their experience but rather to stay committed to lifting their experience up to the level of their belief.

I believe that praying for miracles is dangerous; it's brave and terrifying and defies all that is usual about life in the natural. What about you? Are you still believing for miracles? Are you praying for the impossible and petitioning God for what others deem uncommon, unusual, or unattainable?

For many years, a woman in our church held a position within our leadership team developing community outreach. I remember the day she approached me to tell me that she felt prompted to run for public office. I thought she was crazy. Her faith to gain a seat in our government was not only unusual but also deemed unattainable by people who recognized that she had many circumstances stacked against her. Yet she believed God for what He had spoken to her. She not only won a seat at the next election but held her position for twelve years, gaining the respect of her colleagues and constituents alike for her authenticity and unwavering commitment to bettering the community.

So let me ask you again: are you petitioning God with prayers and requests that others might deem uncommon, unusual, or unattainable? If you're not, I think you should.

Unusual Manifesto

Everything about serving Jesus is unusual, rare, uncommon, and extraordinary. We've already established that His kingdom is an upside-down one and that His call to His followers is a countercultural way.

On the starry night when Christ was born, one of many outrageous assertions were made when a host of angels lit up the night sky and declared, "On earth peace, goodwill toward men!" (Luke 2:14). In a time beset with unrest and marked by rulers who worked for everything *but* peace, this declaration was radical: a new King and a new way was truly born.

Jesus's entire life was marked by unusual encounters and miracles; uncommon grace and mercy defined His presence on earth. The Son of God came into the world with a dangerous declaration. His gospel was a new way, and not only did His Sermon on the Mount leave people in awe of this holy man but the Beatitudes and Lord's Prayer that followed give us a subversive manifesto to live by:

Blessed are those who hunger and thirst for righteousness.

Blessed are those who mourn.

Blessed are the peacemakers.

Blessed are you when you're at the end of your rope.

(see Matthew 5)

At a glance, the Beatitudes seem to be about a life of less—and in many ways they are! They're about less of the meaningless and more of the meaningful, about less of the noise and more of the music, less of the frantic and more of the rest, less of the things that the world says are important and more of what God cares about. In the economy of God, it's all about *how well* and not about *how much.* In the Beatitudes, the emphasis is less about the law and more about grace; it's less about the exterior things and more about the internal (heart issues).

Strange, rare, uncommon, atypical, extraordinary, exceptional, surprising teaching.

Throughout the narration of the world, many such declarations have resonated in hallowed halls or across airwaves and made their way into the history books. Martin Luther King Jr. stood on the steps of the Lincoln Memorial in 1963 and announced, "I have a dream." In 1776, thirteen colonies of America banded together in revolt against the troops of Great Britain and created the Declaration of Independence, which birthed a brand-new nation and ushered in a countercultural way.

Not all declarations, though, are worthy to be repeated. Adolf Hitler declared his political ideologies and power through his prison manifesto, *Mein Kampf,* converting an entire nation to a warped sense of security and an evil narrative.

What does the manifesto of your life declare?

It was a summer's evening and my young grandchildren were running in and out of our house, playing a childlike game of chase right where the huge and heavy solid wood door that adorned our front steps swung open and closed every day. Just moments later, while the kids were safely worn out in the living room, an almighty crash shook the entire first level of our suburban home. We quickly discovered that the giant door—far too heavy for one person to lift—had come completely off its hinges and crashed onto the floorboards below. (We later learned that the door had faulty hinges.) The damage was extensive, but the repercussions could have been so much more devastating if any of the children had been nearby at the time of the collapse.

I believe we live in a world with faulty hinges—a world that can become unhinged at any moment based on people's declarations, both good and bad. Yet we serve a God who is the hinge of history. Without Jesus Christ as the reliable hardware holding fast the ups and downs of each day, all things come unhinged, powerless to hold the weight of a toppling, creaky, and unpredictable swinging door of life and death, good and evil.

Christ can be at the center of your life—secure and carefully placed, swinging closed the door on old, hurtful, and painful things and opening the door on new horizons and plans and purpose. When He is at the center, the manifesto of your life can declare the powerful truth that the way of Christ—even though it is uncommon, unusual, and countercultural—is love, joy, and peace for everyone.

Jesus's declaration will forever enable people to unite around a common cause, the very cause for which He came into the world: that all might have life and have it to the full.

Uncommon People

It was an ordinary day in Jerusalem. I imagine that the sun was beating down on the city gate as the same two friends who had been "troubling the city" walked with one another on their way to the temple. Perhaps they were deep in conversation, discussing what they might preach that afternoon, when they were interrupted by a weary and raspy voice begging for money. Upon closer look, the two men realized that this beggar was also unable to walk. The response of the older disciple was that of a man who expected, despite his shortcomings and humanity, to be used by God. Peter spoke these powerful words: "Silver or gold I do not have, but what I do have I give you. In the name of Jesus Christ of Nazareth, walk" (Acts 3:6, NIV11). In that instant, a crippled beggar was healed and an entire community of religious leaders and officials were astounded that a pair of ordinary, average, and somewhat unusual men could be used by God to perform such a miracle. "When they saw the boldness of Peter and John, and perceived that they were uneducated and untrained men, they marveled. And they realized that they had been with Jesus" (4:13).

In that moment, God confounded the ancient prejudice that you had to be of social stature or nobility to be used by the Lord. It was the simple, ordinary, unusual nature of those He chose to work through that bore testimony to His transforming power and gracious ways.

Have you ever felt unqualified for a life of unusual favor? You ought to know that you are in good company. Not one of Jesus's disciples was qualified! Not only that, but God often uses the common, ordinary, and unusual among us to display His miracle-working power.

It's a sobering thought to consider that Peter and John would not qualify for ministry in many denominations today. They were far too undertrained and undereducated. Training for one's calling shows great wisdom, and education is a huge asset, but ultimately neither can replace the grace of God and the anointing of the Holy Spirit. Almost all the disciples, even Jesus, were from the artisan class and not nobility. Fishermen, canvas workers, and carpenters—they were what Australians call "tradies." They were tradesmen. I encourage you to let God, and no one else, set the boundaries on your life. His ways are exceeding, abundant, and above.

Have you ever heard the name Ananias? Do you know who he was and what he did? Was he a great preacher? An elder, a deacon, or a king? The Scriptures don't tell us anything extraordinary about this man. Acts 22:12 simply says, "He was a devout observer of the law and highly respected by all the Jews living there" (NIV11). But it was Ananias whom God sent to heal Saul—a future apostle—from blindness. It was Ananias who made a way for a remarkable ministry to be brought forth through a whole and healed Saul. An apostle healed by a disciple. Some might say that the ordinary confounded the wise, to echo Saul's (Paul's) later words:

> Brothers and sisters, think of what you were when you were
> called. Not many of you were wise by human standards; not
> many were influential; not many were of noble birth. But God
> chose the foolish things of the world to shame the wise; God
> chose the weak things of the world to shame the strong. God
> chose the lowly things of this world and the despised things—
> and the things that are not—to nullify the things that are, so that
> no one may boast before him. (1 Corinthians 1:26–29, NIV11)

I hope that you expect to be used by God. I pray that despite the fact that you might feel like "only a pastor's wife" or "just an accountant" or "simply a stay-at-home parent" or "a leader of a small ministry," you would know today that God wants to do something unusual and extraordinary with people He puts His hands on, including you. It is in the moments when we feel unqualified, small, and unimportant—in the ordinary, everyday, simple, and quiet moments—that we can choose to allow God to speak to us, breathe in us, and use us for His purpose. Despite our shortcomings, we can choose to open our hands or lift our eyes or reach in our pockets or dig a little deeper to prove that our extraordinary God uses ordinary people—that His ways *are* rare, uncommon, and even sometimes unusual.

Unusual Miracles

The sun was setting in Newport Beach, California, as Bobbie and I sat at a dinner table with our dear friends Nick and Christine Caine, waiting for another couple to join us. We knew Matt and Laurie Crouch, yet even though my television program had been on Trinity Broadcasting Network for many years, we had never really spent much personal time with them. But this was in a year when our whole church was believing for unusual miracles, and that night a *very* big miracle was about to emerge.

Matt is chairman of TBN, and he and Laurie are doing a wonderful job of leading the world's largest Christian network into its second generation and into its future. The meeting almost never happened. There was confusion over what night we had agreed upon, so we sat and waited and waited for them to arrive. Eventually Christine texted Laurie, who was enjoying a movie with Matt, unaware that we were gathering that night. They quickly left the movie and drove straight to the restaurant, where we were just starting our desserts.

Within moments of sitting at the table and exchanging greetings,

Matt leaned over and asked, "Brian, have you ever thought of a Hillsong channel?"

I took a moment to process his question before saying, "Well, yeah, I've thought about it, but . . ." Really, I had thought about only an Australian channel, and we weren't far away from that becoming a reality. But to me, that would have been a miracle without even being able to conceive that God was about to do something much bigger, something beyond what I could ever ask, think, or imagine. I certainly was shocked by the question, but Matt definitely had my complete attention (and giving full attention isn't always my strength).

He then proceeded to tell me about the huge satellite dish they had located just a few miles up the road from where we were eating and directly outside their studios in Tustin. It was a dish that could transmit multiple signals to satellites that then send the signals down to various continents around the world. He talked about how it could work, and for a long time I quizzically wondered whether what I was hearing was what he was actually saying. Was he really inviting us into the Trinity Broadcasting family of networks, to rebrand and creatively reinvent the former Church Channel?

When we finally parted ways, I turned to my friend Nick and asked, "Was he saying what I think he was saying?"

Nick said, "I believe so."

So I asked him to write down in bullet points what was said, to confirm I was hearing right.

Well, fast-forward eight or nine months, many conversations and meetings later, and we entered into a formal business contract marked by the generosity of this couple and the favor of God. A little before 12:00

a.m. on June 1, 2016, I tuned in with tears in my eyes as the countdown started and transmission began at the stroke of midnight. What an extraordinarily unusual miracle!

It still astounds me when I think back to these moments and feel overwhelmed by the unusual miracle. Never in a million years did I imagine a gift of such significance and the opportunity for such influence in the broadcast sector. Today we have a growing team of people who work around the clock to breathe life and hope and encouragement through unique programming and innovative content, beamed 24/7 into the homes of millions of viewers, from the most southern to the far northern parts of the earth. A miracle indeed—and a huge faith step that requires ongoing prayer and support. But it wouldn't have been possible at all if Matt hadn't been obedient to the Holy Spirit and openhandedly generous in his heart.

I've come to realize that most miracles are unusual. Think about the familiar stories of the Bible. When God wanted to deliver His people after the Exodus, He parted the Red Sea. He dried up a path through a huge body of water and then folded it right back into place to defeat the enemy. Joshua 10 tells us about a day like the world has never experienced before or since. The sun stopped so that God's people could have the victory. The Almighty shut the mouths of lions, cooled a fiery furnace, and turned plain water into wine.

I wonder what unusual things God can do in your life—and not only *in* your life but *through* your life also.

The New Testament says that in the time of the apostles, "God gave Paul the power to perform unusual miracles. When handkerchiefs or aprons that had merely touched his skin were placed on sick people, they were healed of their diseases, and evil spirits were expelled" (Acts 19:11–

12, NLT). Like Paul, I want to live a life that points people to Jesus through the gift of unusual miracles. With the Holy Spirit working in me, I want to facilitate the generosity of the Father and be a beacon of salvation, hope, and life that points others to the Son. Don't underestimate what God wants to do in and through you. Don't forget to ask, seek, knock, and desire all the fullness of His gifts and the riches of His will.

I believe that God wants you to enter into your full inheritance as a son or daughter of the Most High. Supernatural, life-transforming miracles are indeed your portion, and God wants to meet you and work through you in the most unusual ways.

Unusual Ways

His name was Mark. It was a horrendous season. He hadn't seen his kids for months after his wife left him for someone else. Not long after this breakdown of his second marriage came his unexpected cancer diagnosis. The weight of life was too much to bear, so Mark decided to end it all. The highest point in the city was a place called Mount Gravatt, and when he punched the location into his GPS, he knew that this would be his final trip.

As he approached Mount Gravatt, traffic slowed to a crawl right at the base of the mountain, as lines of cars wound their way into a large parking lot surrounding an overflowing building. People with friendly faces and fluorescent vests were directing the lines of cars into the large parking lot, and there was a giant sign that read "Welcome Home" scrawled across the oversized entryway. He reluctantly followed. Parking in the designated area, he found there was no way to exit the parking lot, which was overflowing with people, and as he made his way into the building, he muttered under his breath, "God, this is Your last chance." After he was greeted by half a dozen people and then ushered to a seat in the lit-up building at the base of that mountain, his life radically changed in just one night.

Today Mark is a highly dedicated volunteer at our Brisbane Campus, serving every weekend on the venue safety team. His life was in shambles more than three years ago, after his wife left him with a broken heart and after a bleak diagnosis. Never in a million years did he expect to find the lights on at a church at the base of the mountain he was about to throw himself off of, but it was a Friday night and the crowds were overflowing, beckoning him to join. That night, Mark found Jesus at the altar in our ever-growing Brisbane Campus and has since been baptized and restored to relationship with his children.

God sometimes meets us in the most unusual ways. When we are at the end of ourselves is when He is only just beginning. We are called to live unusual lives, called to unusual purpose, and marked for unusual blessing.

On the day when Mark had planned to commit suicide, he felt as though he had nothing to offer life anymore—no skills, no good thing to bring to the table. Now, every single week, he faithfully helps welcome and protect the people in the church he loves—the church where his life was transformed forever.

Exodus 35 details the day Moses gathered all the people and commissioned them to build the tabernacle, just as the Lord had commanded. He procured the help of all kinds of skilled people and encouraged everyone to be involved in this holy work. In verse 35, the writer chronicles the last of the workers to be enlisted: "God has filled them both with unusual skills as jewelers, carpenters, embroidery designers in blue, purple, and scarlet on linen backgrounds, and as weavers—they excel in all the crafts we will be needing in the work" (TLB). *Unusual skills.*

Dear friend, the work of the Lord, the Great Commission, and the call to build His house require everyone to participate. Whatever it is that you uniquely have, bring it to the table with all the passion and enthusiasm you can muster. Decide that your unique strengths and giftings are indeed set apart to do the work of the Lord, and get about doing it, no matter how unusual or uncommon you deem them to be.

In the same way, we must be filled with unusual wisdom and be committed to having unusual influence if we are going to live our lives to the full. Zechariah was a gatekeeper, determining who came inside the city walls and who didn't. The Bible calls him a "man of unusual wisdom" (1 Chronicles 26:14, TLB). I believe that we too must seek God for this kind of wisdom—that leaders, parents, and young people ought to know what and who to let in and what to keep out of their lives. Their destinies are too important to simply let in anything or anyone. Let's believe for unusual wisdom in our daily lives—supernatural, prophetic, instinctive, and intuitive wisdom that defies that which is usual and common.

Be a person committed to listening to the Holy Spirit, learning and discovering the unique ways you've been gifted, and seeking and finding the way the Lord wants you to go.

Uncommon Grace

I suppose this *uncommon grace* makes us wonder, what is *common* grace? Really, the very nature of grace is entirely uncommon. The extravagant love that was shown to us on the cross of Calvary should be the catalyst for the depth and breadth to which we live lives of purpose.

The grace of God is always wasteful (in the best sense of the word) and never deserved, and it is poured out on us over and over again as we make the daily choice to live out of the revelation in Ephesians 3—to trust, obey, and believe for the exceeding, abundant, and above.

As I close this chapter, I want to commission you to pray daring prayers, to make bold declarations, and to believe against all odds for unusual miracles. The love and grace of God demand our best and make a way for us to not only pray for such things but walk in them. From now on, when you believe boldly and courageously for unusual miracles and pray wholeheartedly, as Jesus taught us in Matthew 6:10, "Your will be done," may you understand that His will is more exciting, unusual, wild, and wonderful than even your greatest dreams. As 2 Corinthians 4:7 declares, "We have this treasure in jars of clay to show that this all-surpassing power is from God and not from us" (NIV11).

It's not about the ordinary vessel, the common container; it's about the uncommon grace and unusual favor God has bestowed upon us. The price Jesus paid is worthy of our best, and this unique, uncommon, unusual, extraordinary, rare, and dangerous declaration that we carry needs a church and a people who are going to give their very lives to see it come to pass.

12

New Roads and New Rivers

Are you a sunset person or a sunrise person? Do you live on the east coast or the west coast? (Or as our tunnel-visioned Hillsong NYC team members love to phrase it, the west coast or the *best* coast?) Of course, not everyone lives near the water, so I wonder what a sunrise or sunset looks like for you. Whether it's a desert plain or a mountain range welcoming the rising sun or bidding farewell to the final rays, what a beautiful canvas the sun continuously paints in the sky!

Sydney is situated on Australia's east coast, and we are luxuriously afforded one magnificent beach after another along our coastline. I have no complaints that this is the city Bobbie and I were called to move to forty years ago. It's the "exceeding, abundant, and above" that God has graced us with.

And it's in Sydney's eastern suburbs that I've been blessed to wake up many times to a golden sunrise on Bondi Beach, a world-renowned half moon of silky sand and crashing waves. On this beautiful stretch of creation, if you wake up early enough on a clear day, you will see God's beauty personified in the form of an iconic Australian sunrise.

As the night is about to surrender to early morning light, first an almost undetectable line forms on the horizon, and then as that linear impression brightens, it changes shape and becomes an undeniable glow that somehow declares there is so much more to come. Sure enough, suddenly golden beams peek above the horizon. Beautifully radiant and laced with purpose, they move determinedly into view, announcing that a new day has dawned.

What about you? Have you peered beyond your bedroom curtains recently to recognize the vibrancy on the horizon at the break of dawn or the sunlight dancing through the trees, casting shadows on the walls? Every single sunrise is different. Every single day brings something new. Have you pulled to the side of the road lately and inhaled a deep breath, drinking in the freshness of a new day dawning, and remembered—with gratitude—that every day with Jesus is filled with new life, new opportunity, new grace and goodness? The Bible says it so beautifully:

> Behold, I will do a new thing,
> Now it shall spring forth;
> Shall you not know it?
> I will even make a road in the wilderness
> And rivers in the desert. (Isaiah 43:19)

So, what does it look like to walk along new roads and travel new rivers?

A New Thing

Each of us needs newness. We crave it and must continually seek out the new to replace and refresh the old. We've discussed what it looks like to break free from old habits and what it takes to find an anchored faith, calling, and consistency in Christ.

But what's next? What does a "new thing" look like for you? Did you know that God longs to do a new thing in and through you, not just once but every single day?

Perhaps you need supernatural intervention. Maybe the "new thing" for you looks like breakthrough in this season. I have good news: we serve a God of breakthrough. Not only did God deliver the children of Israel out of captivity in Egypt by "breaking through" the Red Sea, but He intervened on their behalf time and time again when they needed it most. He brought them freedom from captivity, provision when they had nothing, and answers to their prayers when they were at the end of themselves. Both freedom and provision are promises that accompany a new thing. In what area of your life do you need supernatural breakthrough or God's intervention or provision and freedom? Remember, He is the God of more.

Maybe the new thing you have your eyes and heart set upon requires the favor of God. Once again, He is the God of favor. He gave the children of Israel favor with Pharaoh, which led to a roadway of freedom and provision in the wilderness. He gave His people favor with Cyrus, the Persian ruler of Babylon, who allowed them to not only return to their land but also rebuild the temple. It was favor from the most unexpected and unlikely source. Could you imagine the president of Iran funding a

Christian ministry in Jerusalem today? That is exactly the kind of miracle it was!

Our God remains the God of favor. Isaiah says it best:

The Lord [earnestly] waits [expecting, looking, and longing] to be gracious to you; and therefore He lifts Himself up, that He may have mercy on you and show loving-kindness to you. For the Lord is a God of justice. Blessed (happy, fortunate, to be envied) are all those who [earnestly] wait for Him, who expect and look and long for Him [for His victory, His favor, His love, His peace, His joy, and His matchless, unbroken companionship]! (Isaiah 30:18, AMPC)

The Lord wants to favor you and shower His mercy upon you. His companionship can be the source of blessing and fullness in your life that you never could have imagined, and simply staying on the path of relationship with Jesus is all that it requires.

In chapters 9, 10, and 11, we discussed the roadblocks, trouble, and miracles that mark the journey with Christ. But I love the conversation God has with Moses in Exodus when this tired leader relays the fears and hesitations of his people to the Father. God's response to him is this: "Why do you cry to Me? Tell the children of Israel to go forward" (14:15). Maybe you too have reached an end. Maybe you also long for something new but have found the road to be bumpy. God always has a way forward; you just need to keep moving. He is always true to His Word, and as we just read, His Word declares new roads and new rivers.

Declarations

Isaiah 43 is filled with declarations that pertain to our future. God sees you. He knows you. He cares for you and cares for the things you care about.

I love the testimonies from little children that share the wonder they feel when they pray for and receive something like a puppy. Or when someone prays for a parking spot. Perhaps you scoff at the idea that the God of the universe cares about such trivial things, but I don't. I believe that He is so invested in our lives, so committed to our well-being, our present and our future, that He loves to lavish on us reminders of His goodness. Reminders like these:

"I've Got This"
Verse 15 of Isaiah 43 says,

> I am the LORD, your Holy One,
> The Creator of Israel, your King.

Before He made His promise in verses to come, God declared His ultimate title: I AM. He immediately followed that up with four others: the Lord, the Holy One, Creator, and King. In other words, He is well able to a do a new thing.

What are you believing God for this year or next? Can you see it in your heart and in your mind's eye? God's got it. You can trust Him. Are you going to release your faith and take hold of His promises for your life? Are you going to jump into the new thing with both feet, knowing full well that His titles as Shepherd, Savior, Friend, and King are not merely words but poignant declarations of His power and ability to direct, rescue, comfort, and lead you safely into new seasons and to new horizons?

"I've Done This Before"

Verse 16 says,

> Thus says the LORD, who makes a way in the sea
> And a path through the mighty waters.

It's not just poetry. God is prompting us again to remember that He alone makes a way, a path through the impassable. He did it before for the Israelites, and He will do it again for you.

Why do we read out praise reports and testimonies in church? Because sometimes we need to be reminded that He has done for others the very same thing that you are asking Him to do for you. He *still* provides miracles, *still* breathes life into dead things, and will *still* hold back mighty waters and rushing seas to free His people. He is qualified to handle the dreams and desires of your heart, and He wants to reassure you and me that we can trust Him with even the impossible things.

"I'm Going to Do It Again"

The last of God's three amazing declarations to remind us of His goodness is this:

> Do not remember the former things,
> Nor consider the things of old. (verse 18)

Forget the disappointments, regrets, and losses of the past. Cast them from your mind! Get your gaze up, onto the horizon, and envision the new day dawning.

In the same way that it is common to revert our attention to failures of the past, it's far too easy to allow our sentiment to erode significance. Significance is about the future and all that is ahead, but sentiment is about the former things. If you are the kind of person who looks back on the "glory days," can I encourage you to remember that your significance is in what is ahead of you, not what is behind you? God says He is going to do a new thing. "Now it shall spring forth" (verse 19). Do you expect God to do a new thing in your life? Are you looking ahead to where it is? The new thing is not behind you, my friend, but it is most certainly ahead.

I have always chuckled at people who have been in church at Hillsong for a long time and refer to twenty years ago as "the good ol' days." Although we have had so many high points along the way, there have never been days like the ones we are enjoying right now. Oh sure, we had some fun and God did amazing things in our midst in the past, but I don't ever want to go back there! In the last twenty years, we have seen exponential growth and countless lives changed and communities transformed.

My team members laugh at me when I mention how I love to settle into my comfy chair after a full Sunday in church and tune in to *Precious Memories,* a gospel television show that takes me straight down memory lane as I sing along to the old songs we sang in church back at a time when we called worship "the choruses," with only pastors leading, waving their arms like a conductor. The Gaither Vocal Band often buoys my spirits as I lean back and sing along to the familiar tunes. But even though

I enjoy *Precious Memories* for sentimental reasons, I'm not the type to hanker after the past for too long. When I say the best is yet to come, I mean it. For the most part, the good old days weren't quite as good as we seem to remember them having been. Aging people, in particular, need to guard against camping in the past and reflecting on moments that their memories have inflated as the years have gone by. I do love to reminisce and share a laugh with good friends, but my focus is continuously forward.

When Isaiah prophesied that God would do a new thing, he was exhorting people not to be looking back to former things or old things—the things that took place through the miraculous deliverance of God's people from Egypt as Moses led them through the parting sea. He was reminding them that there could be miraculous deliverance in Babylon, too—that He could still change the hearts of kings and bring new roads of faith and rivers of provision to their current circumstances.

I want to celebrate the past, but I don't want to live there. I want to keep my eyes on the future, ever expectant, watching for the next thing, the new thing that God is about to do.

Roads and Rivers

When God spoke through the prophet Isaiah and declared that He would do a new thing, He then went on to explain that the new thing was making "a road in the wilderness and rivers in the desert" (Isaiah 43:19). What a picture! Other translations speak of "a pathway through the wilderness" (NLT) and "rivers in the badlands" (MSG). The new thing—the God thing—brings life where there was none. It also brings new vivacity where perhaps old growth has lost momentum. The new thing, just like the sunrise, shines light on our comfort. It exposes the dust on the ground and begs us to wash the windows. It enables us to open our eyes and see something monotonous with fresh life and new colors, to rid our hearts of cobwebs and our souls of stagnation.

I appreciate long-term friends—the stick-with-you-every-step-of-the-way kind of friends. There's a depth in relationship that can be forged only by traveling a lot of miles together. Steve Penny is one of those friends for me. He has been a ministry colleague and a friend for a long time now. He's a unique character who has a gift of encouragement thinly camouflaged under a layer of friendly bravado.

When we met in January 2015 for our annual holiday breakfast together at Aromas café in beautiful Noosa, Queensland (a destination that Bobbie and I have loved for a long time), Steve began to speak to me about new roads and new rivers. This breakfast at the beginning of January is a tradition we have kept for years now, and often it is during these meetings that Steve's musings and prophetic gift minister to me personally. As Steve began to share his revelation about Isaiah 43, it resonated so strongly within me that I knew I had to speak it boldly over our church that year.

It's an important declaration. You see, roads take you to new horizons, new possibilities, and new opportunities. And rivers are a source of supply, provision, and resource. My prayer for you is that as you discover more of the character of God and His desire for you to flourish and grow, you will find yourself traveling new roads and new rivers.

It's a common but true metaphor that life is a pathway, a journey we take along the roads and seasons of growth, opportunity, and experience. As we know, these roads of life are rarely straight, flat, and wide like a freeway—at least not for very long!

Proverbs 15:24 says, "The way of life winds upward for the wise." That image makes me think of a winding road that leads up to a mountain peak. You can't see very far ahead because the road bends and twists with steep and narrow paths. On roads like this, you may need to stop for rest in order to regain the strength to continue. This road is for "the wise," who understand that their lives have purpose that unfolds along the way. And the higher one goes, the better the perspective!

It's not always the easiest of climbs, but remember, the view at the top is always magnificent! Does that mean something to you? Is there a pathway you are setting upon or a new thing on the horizon that feels a little out of reach? Don't be discouraged. God makes a way. Stick with the journey through all its twists and turns.

The truth of nature and genius of our Creator is that often an upward-winding road follows the path of a river flowing down. In God's economy, where there are roads, there are rivers. With God's purpose comes His provision. It's no good to have new roads of opportunity without the rivers of provision for the journey.

The Bible has a lot to say about rivers. For example, Jesus declared, "If anyone thirsts, let him come to Me and drink. He who believes in Me, as the Scripture has said, out of his heart will flow *rivers of living water*" (John 7:37–38).

Ezekiel 47:1–12 speaks of rivers that flow from the temple, bringing life to everything as they wind their way into the Dead Sea. Many years ago, Bobbie and I visited the country of Jordan and had the opportunity to swim in the Dead Sea, which is a geographic wonder. It is the most depressed spot on earth, and rivers continuously flow into this stagnant body of water. Although I marveled at the biblical and historical significance of where we found ourselves, it was not an experience I thoroughly enjoyed. It's not called the Dead Sea for nothing. It's hard to describe the strangeness of involuntarily floating virtually *on* the surface of the water, and the level of saltiness that burns your eyes, nose, mouth, and every other part of you if you are not careful. Despite the warnings to keep my eyes closed, I somehow managed to get the toxic waters in them. Excruciating! And as our Arabic pastor friends from Amman showed us, the Dead Sea experience would not be complete until we joined hundreds of people sitting on the muddy shores and covering ourselves from head to toe with the supposedly "healing" brown silt.

When I think of rivers flowing down from the temple in Jerusalem—a city perched high in the hills—and down to the earth's lowest point, bringing instant life to whatever it touches, it really does paint a vivid picture in my mind. What flows out of the house of God, the church, should also touch dead things and bring them to life. Rivers have living water; the very nature of them is constant motion and change. Much like a river, the gospel was never intended to be contained; it was always intended to be shared.

Similarly, Micah 4:1 paints a picture of a river of people flowing *into* the temple. When it comes to the house of God, we must continuously believe for people to flow in and for life to flow out. I desire to see the kind of life flowing from our churches that touches sin and poverty, injustice and sickness, and brings help, healing, and new life to dead things. I pray that our lives and our churches will be road maps to salvation, a testimony of His faithfulness and the source of endless rivers of life and healing to others.

A life in Christ has new roads of purpose and vision and new rivers of life and provision along the way. Have faith; keep your eyes on the horizon! Don't be discouraged if the new roads bring new challenges, because new roads of faith will always release new rivers of blessing.

Challenge

When God makes a declaration, there is often a challenge connected with it. And the challenge usually boils down to this: *Will you believe it?* In this passage of Isaiah 43 we've been looking at, God's challenge to Israel and to us today is, *Can you believe I will do this for you?*

As followers of Christ, we are called to lift our beliefs above what we see with our natural eyes to what God declares in His Word to be truth. Second Corinthians 5:7 sums it up: "We walk by faith, not by sight." To embrace all that God has planned for your life, you must lay hold of His promise to make a way for you through the wilderness and the valleys.

Many years ago, when Bobbie and I first came to Sydney, we had no clue what God would do or what was ahead. All we had to go on were God's promises and the dreams of our hearts. The call of God is truly an adventure, with plenty of challenges and not much clarity about what lies ahead, other than the fact that what He has promised us is going to be good! So we need to settle in our hearts that it is a journey navigated by faith, not by sight. Remember, wherever God leads you, He provides the way for you to reach your destination.

I'm asking you again, are you believing for the new thing? New life for your work, new energy for your day, new provision for your future, and new grace for the journey? I know there is more ahead of you, and I know the road can seem bumpy, the landscape vast, and the climate dry.

But we serve the God of more and the God of the new thing. And I once heard someone say, "The best is yet to come." Do you believe it?

Stand in Awe and Be Amazed

This chapter has focused on God's declaration "Behold, I will do a new thing" (Isaiah 43:19). Do you know what *behold* means? It actually means to "stand in awe and be amazed." In modern parlance, it's saying, "Wow!"

So, why did God say this? What was He trying to get our attention for? I believe that His announcement was a statement of His character: *I am a Redeemer.* The declaration that He wanted His people to stand in awe and be amazed was not just for their own benefit; it was also to announce hope for humanity through Jesus Christ and the grace of the gospel.

As He spoke a faith path out of the Israelites' seventy-year captivity into liberation and redemption, God was calling His people out from the old and into the new. He was calling things that were not yet as though they had already happened. As far as God was concerned, it was already a done deal.

Today I believe that the Lord would say to us, "Behold! I am doing a new thing." He is calling us to come up and out of the ordinary and rise above our perceived limits. He is asking us to *see* and *respond* to His hand of preparation and purpose in our lives and in the church, His bride—to behold what He has done, is doing, and will continue to do as we live righteously, according to the Word of God and with a vision to see His kingdom come here on earth.

Are you expecting God to do a new thing in your life right now?

That may seem overwhelming when you consider your present circumstances, but take courage and let me remind you that the Bible declares that God has already made a way, carved a road to lead you, and positioned rivers of provision to refresh you. "If anyone thirsts, let him *come* to me and drink. Rivers of living water will brim and spill out of the depths of anyone who believes in me this way, just as the Scripture says" (John 7:38, MSG).

So much is on the horizon of your life. So much lies ahead in waiting. Don't be discouraged by bumps in the road or detours on the path. Jesus is in the details. Continue to trust, put your faith in God, and speak *new* things into wilderness or desert seasons. Taste and see what God is doing in your life, in your endeavors, and across the world and be amazed.

What dreams and desires, hopes and miracles, prayers and petitions are bubbling over within you as you read this? Do you expect it? Can you lay hold of it? Shall you not know it? It's invisible and it's unexplainable, but it is born of God, and the day is coming when these dreams and desires will spring up because He knows them and declares them even *before* they do.

Second Corinthians 5:17 testifies to the new thing that God has begun and is doing: "If anyone is in Christ, he is a new creation; old things have passed away; behold, all things have become new." Don't underestimate the amazing things God has placed in you and what they can become when they spring forth. What are you beholding? We become like what we behold. If you are looking fully into God's face, seeking His heart, and living according to His will, then that is where the new and miraculous—the *wow*—is going to come from. That is the place from which your stand-in-awe-and-be-amazed moments will spring forth.

I want you to expect new roads of opportunity, new possibilities, unusual miracles, and new horizons in places yet untouched. I want you to expect more than you can ask, dream, think, or imagine. Believe that God is opening up new heights where you will have an amazing perspective and orchestrating new sunrises that cause you to throw open the windows with expectation for what God is about to do.

The way of the righteous is like the first gleam of dawn,
which shines ever brighter until the full light of day.
(Proverbs 4:18, NLT)

Stand in awe and be amazed.

13

Ceilings and Floors

Think about the Chicago Bulls basketball team for a minute and which is the first name that springs to mind? Remember the Nike swoosh and a silhouetted figure—the ball perfectly poised, soaring high above the basket, and a man, head and shoulders above the rest. Whose name would you utter? If crowds were asked, "Who was the greatest basketball player of all time?" undoubtedly the name Michael Jordan would be on most people's lips. He was a true superstar, an icon of the game. His name is recognizable even by people who care little for athletics, such was this sporting legend's fame.

In 2009, Michael Jordan was inducted into the Basketball Hall of Fame, and though his athleticism was never in question, his enshrinement speech showed a side to the man that may have surprised many. He was known to be unbelievably competitive, but during the twenty minutes he spoke, Jordan addressed his sons and said that he "felt sorry for them."* Jordan mused that they could never live up to the bar that was set by their celebrity father, the standard of competition he enjoyed in his

---

* Jon Greenberg, "The Man Behind the Legend," *ESPN,* September 12, 2009, www.espn.com/chicago/columns/story?columnist=greenberg_jon&id=4468210.

glory days, and remarked on the constant shadow that they must live under. Perhaps with his expertise, he could see the limitations in their skill sets, but I don't think I would have liked to be one of his boys that day. Maybe they were never created to be basketball legends. Maybe they were gifted in other areas where they too could reach the very top.

I don't know about you, but as a father, I never want to cast a shadow on my children. It is my hope and prayer that my kids will do far greater things than I ever did—that they will see more than I saw and experience greater success and blessing, reaching taller peaks than I ever could. My desire is that, just as they did when they were small children, they would (metaphorically) climb onto my back, knowing that my shoulders are broad and strong enough not simply to hold their weight but to hoist them higher and launch them into whatever new endeavors and exciting adventures their journey might take them on.

Our heavenly Father desires the same.

There are no limits to His love, no jealousy in His way, and no impossible expectations that He has placed upon our shoulders. He longs for humanity to tell a story of victory, for old and young to work and live together harmoniously, and for generations to relay the faithfulness of their fathers and the sacrifices of those gone before.

It is my single greatest prayer that my ceilings will be the next generation's floor.

Fathers and Sons

Sadly, some fathers are sufficiently dysfunctional to leave their children struggling with the fallout of the hurt and conflict that they themselves endured all through their lives. Of course, every one of us fathers has made a few mistakes along the way. But when I think of functional, healthy fathers, I think of the seasoned, proven, known, established, experienced, and safe.

In contrast, sons are untested, unproven, uninitiated, untried, and much riskier bets. There is so much to be said for wisdom that comes with age and experience and plenty to be said for the wide-eyed wonder, curiosity, and innovation of younger generations.

My sons are risk takers, much more so than I am today. It would take a lot of coaxing to get me in the water during a southerly swell, when the waves are reaching higher than my house. But my sons see big waves as an opportunity they can't resist, racing to put on their wet suits and get into the frothy waters with their surfboards.

When Joel and Ben were still teenagers, they were passionate snowboarders, and I made a brave decision at almost fifty years of age to switch from being an average skier to a below-average snowboarder. My main reason for the change was to spend more time with my sons, but the moment they took me to the highest and steepest trail on the mountain, telling me to "just go down," before disappearing between the trees, it became clear I would never keep up with them, even though my capabilities slowly improved.

We can learn so much from a generation of risk takers—young people who see the future ahead of them as being long and inviting. The church will always benefit from the leadership of men and women who are untainted by the disappointments of life, unobstructed by the ways of the past, and unfazed by the challenges ahead.

Jesus confronted old ways of thinking and irrelevant practices when He said, "No one puts new wine into old wineskins; otherwise the wine will burst the skins, and the wine is lost and the skins as well; but one puts new wine into fresh wineskins" (Mark 2:22, NASB). Nowadays, with our fancy bottles and continual access to fresh water, it's hard to imagine the need to carry a goatskin around in our bag. But in Jesus's day, the skins of goats were stitched tight and used to transport both water and wine. When new wine was placed in a wineskin, it would stretch with ease and flexibility, but too much new wine in an already stretched wineskin would cause it to burst, spilling the contents onto the ground.

Similarly, we can tend to get our hearts stuck on certain ways of doing things. Some churches and entire denominations resist any form of change or reinvention, believing that what is tried, proven, and tested is always the road to travel.

Although the message of the gospel and truth of God's Word are timeless, the methods by which we serve them to our world must continuously shift and change or else risk "bursting." Stale religious systems, terminology, and rituals must be replaced with relevant, sometimes untried methods and music to draw in a new crowd and attract the next generation, moving forward from our old ways into the future. But many churches and ministries today insist on pouring their new wine into the old models again and again, resisting innovation and fighting progress.

As I was growing up, we consistently sang out of the Elim *Redemption Hymnal* in our church. "Turn to number 163" was a common call, and every week, we would rely on the red hardcover books found directly in front of us, behind the forward pew. As a kid, I turned everything into a competition, so I would while away the time as the preacher pounded out his sermon, by counting the number of songs each author had written to see who had the most melodies included. You will be pleased to know that it was a close call between Charles Wesley and Fanny J. Crosby.

The thing is, I liked many of those songs and thank God for the blessing of old hymns that can still be enjoyed. But I'm not living there, and I'm grateful that we have moved on and received a new song from the Lord. We are called to be about the future, called to be moving forward. The Word of God remains, but some things must change. As a younger pastor, I placed little value on tradition, but as the years have rolled on, I've developed a greater appreciation for some traditions and can see how liturgy has its place among our worship. As a matter of fact, I believe that healthy contemporary churches can have their own liturgy, or order of service. But it's just a pity when the Holy Spirit is locked out of His own house because we are so stuck in our ways.

What about you? Do you resist change? Are you comfortable with what has always been—happy to rest in the safety of what you've always done and already tried? Indeed, most of us feel so much better about the proven, tested, and tried. But I believe that the Lord is calling a generation of people to lift the ceiling on what has been—to move away from what is safe and established and expect more from the God who is always doing something new. Resisting change can actually hold us back from experiencing some of these facets of God. Change, though sometimes scary, leads us into a deeper faith walk and communion with our Creator. In moments of uncertainty, we lean on the One who is always certain and never changing—the One who can lead us into a life above all we could ask, think, or imagine.

I see so much hope for the future, and I believe I am called to set up the next generations to be all God has called them to be. I want to see the kingdom advancing in my life, and I want it all the more as I advance in age. No matter what decade of your life you find yourself in, I believe that you too must keep pushing toward the untried, because if there is one thing I have learned in years of leadership, it is that experience is not everything.

Think Bigger

I think experience is overrated. For example, there are people with so much more experience than I have at being married—after all, I've been married only once. There are people more experienced than I at pastoring churches, as I've been pastoring the same one for almost all my adult years. I don't say that with any sense of smugness. I'm simply making the point that experience in and of itself doesn't mean we have learned anything from it, and sometimes we can sometimes produce negative fruit. Cynicism can build a case for telling our own children or those we lead what can't be done, simply because "we've tried it before and it didn't work."

In a town called Antioch of Pisidia, Paul the apostle preached a stirring sermon that was met by cynicism from some of those hardened Jews who had gathered in the synagogue to hear him. Although many who were gathered were eager to hear from this anointed man and would even invite him back so they could discover more of the gospel story, others stood back with folded arms. That day, hundreds of people heard things they had never heard in all their religious experience. With amazement, they began to see that through Jesus Christ, there was so much more for them. But examine again the verse we read in chapter 7 of this book, when Paul addressed the cynics in the crowd with a direct challenge:

Watch out, cynics;
Look hard—watch your world fall to pieces.
I'm doing something right before your eyes
That you won't believe, though it's staring you in the face.
    (Acts 13:41, MSG)

There you have it! Are there possibilities or opportunities staring you in the face that you can't see because they exceed your realm of possibility? Are there things you react to with cynicism because they are far beyond anything you have ever experienced or seen? Maybe things you have known or experienced in the past undermine the possibility of God doing something fresh and new. Yes, we can build others through all we have experienced, but our experience can be built on only what is established or the things we have already learned and already know. There is so much to be said about embracing the new and diving into the unknown.

I may have said a time or two that we value heritage and we honor and recognize the past, but we must continually press on and look to the future. I am grateful for my heritage. I am thankful that I was raised in the church and was surrounded with the things of God. But I am also grateful that my parents never held me back from the new places, new ways, and new opportunities that God was calling me to.

We have a mission statement at Hillsong that speaks of "empowering people to lead and impact in every sphere of life." The truth is, you will never inspire people to have an impact if you don't have a spirit of release and a spirit that is comfortable with the unpredictable. If you think that doing life with Jesus is predictable, you are wrong. It is always an adventure!

Jesus was the king of unpredictability. According to John 4, He astounded people by speaking to someone He never should have been talking to. He stopped to minister to a woman, and not just any woman— a Samaritan woman! His ministry was constantly unpredictable, often angered the religious in the crowds, and astonished His own disciples. They could hardly keep up. Why was He talking to an unclean Gentile woman—a sinful woman? What water was He talking about when He told her she would never thirst again? Why was He bothering with her when the disciples had already gone ahead to eat? What an unpredictable end to their day! Yes, there was nothing predictable about following Jesus.

When my kids were young and I would travel frequently, one of my favorite things to do was arrange to fly home a day or two early and surprise them. Their faces said it all as I strolled in the front door a full twenty-four hours before they were expecting me and then took them to school or spent a day with them after a long time apart.

I believe that our lives and our churches are also called to be predictably unpredictable—that conventional wisdom, established thought, public opinion, peer pressure, and majority thinking can quench the new blessing that God longs to bring into our lives. Can I encourage you? Bring your children up with spontaneity. Open your heart to new experiences—new ways of learning and leading. Live more loyally to the future than to the past. Keep looking forward to all that God has for you, and don't be surprised when He intentionally calls you to shake the dust off your feet and pushes you forward into unpredictability.

The Friend Known as Predictability

Although I believe unpredictability (not impulsiveness or compulsiveness) can be an asset, there are clearly times when predictability is your friend. As unpredictable as life with Jesus could be for the disciples, when it came to serving the will of His Father and fulfilling the purpose of His incarnate existence, Jesus was remarkably predictable. In your life too there are many areas in which predictability will hold you in good stead. Moving forward into the far-above-what-you-could-ever-ask-or-imagine life also means being resolute in your character and constantly growing in stature and favor with both God and man. The following predictable qualities will aid you in that endeavor.

Loyalty

Live in a way that allows people to predict your loyalty. Be a trustworthy companion, a listening ear, and someone who is not constantly moved by changing tides and the shifting circumstances of life.

> Don't lose your grip on Love and Loyalty.
> Tie them around your neck; carve their initials on
> your heart.
> Earn a reputation for living well
> in God's eyes and the eyes of the people.
> (Proverbs 3:3–4, MSG)

Reliability

Being reliable goes hand in hand with being credible. Your boss, your family, and your friends need to know that you are reliable—that you are predictable in your commitment to be there and do what you said you were going to do. Don't be unpredictable when it comes to showing up. Reliability will reassure others that you are someone they can count on and the person to call when either adversity or opportunity knocks.

Belief

Do you know what you believe? Do you know the foundations of your faith? We have foundational beliefs at Hillsong about the Cross, the Resurrection, and the Holy Spirit. In order to move forward and make a difference for the kingdom of God, we must be resolute in our beliefs—not chasing fads or wishy-washy in our stance on Bible issues but confident in both *who* and *what* we believe in.

Even while he was in prison, Paul said, "I know whom I have believed and am persuaded that He is able to keep what I have committed to Him" (2 Timothy 1:12). He wasn't allowing his circumstances to sway his belief. He was confident in what he knew to be true and resolute to share it.

Commitment

It's not a popular word these days. So many people are good starters, but too many are not good finishers. We can all get excited at the beginning of the year—confident in our resolutions and committed to change. But it's not how you start that matters but how you finish. Let's be predictable when it comes to our commitments.

Keeping Your Word

Matthew 5:37 says, "Let your 'Yes' be 'Yes' and your 'No' be 'No'" (WEB). We should be old-fashioned enough that our word is better than a contract.

Be honest in your dealings and straightforward in your communication. Don't give people any room to assume that you are not telling the truth or that *yes* only means *maybe* and that *no* is *perhaps not*. Honesty will propel you forward into your God-given destiny.

Vision

A highlight for our church every year is Vision Sunday, when we stream and connect to well over one hundred thousand people in the nineteen countries where Hillsong Church exists. People arrive excited for the presentation and the message from God that sets our course and rallies our faith for the year immediately ahead. But funnily enough, it's not always easy to say something different, because we don't change our vision every year. We set the vision for Hillsong Church more than thirty-four years ago. Since then, it has grown; we make new announcements. But from a big picture perspective, we've served the same vision all these years and are still on the same course. In another way, it is easy to speak again about our vision, because it is still fresh in our hearts. We lift our eyes higher but stay grounded in what we know that God called us to all those years ago.

Realize who and what you are about. Don't be easily swayed off course or discouraged. Live with a vision that is attached to the cause of King Jesus and watch Him take you to places you never could have imagined.

Fresh and Flourishing

No matter what age you find yourself currently, there is room in the kingdom of God for everyone to make a contribution:

> It shall come to pass in the last days, says God,
> That I will pour out of My Spirit on all flesh;
> Your sons and your daughters shall prophesy,
> Your young men shall see visions,
> Your old men shall dream dreams. (Acts 2:17)

Jesus gave the Great Commission to the church more than two thousand years ago, and it hasn't aged! He didn't put a limit on age, race, creed, or culture; He simply commissioned each of us to go about building the kingdom.

People have asked me when I'm going to retire. The truth is, I am well into my sixties and have never felt better. I'm not winding down my life; I'm turning the vision up!

The kingdom of God is generational. The Word of God is generational. It was Abraham, then Isaac, and then Jacob. The New Testament starts with a genealogy of Jesus containing forty-two generations in all, and in God's master plan, it was fourteen generations from Abraham to David, fourteen more generations from King David to the captivity of the Israelites in Babylon, then fourteen further generations to Jesus Christ. The Word of God says, "One generation will declare Your works to the next" (Psalm 145:4, HCSB), and I'm not done declaring!

Since I was a kid, I had it in my heart that I was called to one day lead our movement of churches, the Australian Christian Churches. At the age of thirty-six, I became president of our state organization, and at the age of forty-three, I was voted in as the ACC national president.

Some people wonder why I would take all that extra responsibility on, and sometimes I asked myself the same question. For twelve years, I served a growing movement of more than eleven-hundred self-governing churches; then I felt that God was calling me to a new season with the promise that it would be a step forward, not a step back. I would be lying to say that I didn't feel a little displaced for a few weeks, but I quickly moved on, as I knew this was not the pinnacle of my life. What's more, the past nine years of my life—when I could have easily felt irrelevant or "past my time"—have been by far the most influential, fruitful, and enjoyable years of my life. So much so that I shake my head in disbelief at just how faithful our God is.

Essentially, I was always looking further down the road, and you can never feel threatened about leaving old seasons behind if you're lifting your eyes higher and seeing exciting new horizons ahead for yourself:

> The righteous shall flourish like a palm tree,
> He shall grow like a cedar in Lebanon.
> Those who are planted in the house of the LORD
> Shall flourish in the courts of our God.
> They shall still bear fruit in old age;
> They shall be fresh and flourishing. (Psalm 92:12–14)

Take it from me: no matter what stage of life you are in, your time isn't over yet. The old adage "Where there's life, there's hope" is certainly true in this wonderful adventure called faith!

Legacy Left and Legacy Lived

It is my heart's desire that as long as God gives me breath, I will continue to lead by example. I want to be intentional about raising up new leaders—young leaders who will bring something fresh and innovative to our team. I want to give young people permission to be all that God has called them to be and constantly give them the opportunities to prove themselves. But too many leaders feel threatened by or fail to trust young leaders. They are fearful to give up authority and end up with a graying church or an aging group of people who lack creativity and forward movement. Sadly, that will almost certainly lead to a focus on "the glory years" and more than a few empty seats. I love to see the pews filled with people of every age, from young people to those who contribute silver-haired wisdom.

Instead of Your fathers shall be Your sons,
Whom You shall make princes in all the earth. (Psalm 45:16)

In that spirit, I believe that it is my job as a leader to be both a room giver and a roof lifter when it comes to the next generation. I want to be a kingmaker, making space for others to grow taller and enlarge their capacity and influence. But you can never lift a ceiling that you can't reach yourself. So in order to raise other people's ceilings, your own life and leadership will require consistent stretching and growing.

King Solomon's heart wasn't in a good place when he asked, "Why do I just work hard for others to enjoy the fruit?" (see Ecclesiastes 2:21). In his backslidden state, he could see no point in working so hard when it would be others who would receive the blessing. But when I look to the church, that is exactly why I believe we are here: to set up younger people to do greater things and take longer strides than we ever could. I've always believed that if God's kingdom is working right, the generations should be getting stronger, one generation building on the foundations of another.

As a pastor, I love seeing God work generationally. At Hillsong, we dedicate babies once every month, and what a joy it is, after more than thirty years of pastoring the same church, to be dedicating the babies of babies I dedicated many years before. It's the kingdom at work, breathing life into a new Jesus generation.

The exceedingly-above-all-you-can-ask-or-imagine life is as much about having a legacy in others as it is about you, and legacy is just as much about now as it is about the future. *Legacy left* can be defined by material and temporal wealth (assets and reputation), but *legacy lived* is relational and based on bringing purpose into the here and now, depositing timeless values into generations to come.

I want to make history, not serve history. I want to learn from history while not repeating history's mistakes. I honor history, those who have gone before me and on whose shoulders I stand, but I do not intend to be contained by history and a misguided loyalty to the limitations of generations past.

I want to defy the odds of history rather than find myself boxed in by its limitations. And I want to carve out new history and not just remember history's "good old days" or its failures and disappointments.

What will your legacy, and the generations that follow, say about you? When asked this question, the great English prime minister Winston Churchill replied, "History will be kind to me, for I intend to write it myself."† I want to encourage you to "write your history" in a way that speaks to the generational nature of our God. Constantly look to the future, sow seeds of opportunity for others, and live a life that raises the ceiling on every limitation that holds you back.

Dancing on the Ceiling

Life with Christ is always about looking forward—setting our eyes on the future and being confident in the hope we have that there is more to

---

† Winston Churchill, quoted in John M. Martin, "Winston Churchill's Cold War," Library of Congress Information Bulletin 62, no. 1 (January 2003), www.loc.gov/loc/lcib/0301/churchill .html.

this life than what we can currently see. Our opportunities, decisions, and blessings today are not simply about us; they are about releasing others into their God-given destinies.

My definition of success is building a platform for future generations to win. God has graced me, metaphorically, with a wonderful floor to build upon, set up by the generation before so that I can step out and serve Him. But ultimately I want my ceilings to be the floors on which my own sons' and daughter's generation will dance—floors that set a foundation for the ceilings to lift off lives and advance the kingdom for generations to come.

14

Spiritually Dead and Spiritually Alive

Airport anxiety—is there such a thing? Traveling internationally is a monthly, if not weekly, task for me these days. With Hillsong churches in multiple countries and continents, airports sometimes feel like my second home. I have long had an aversion to immigration lines and customs officers. Now, it's not that I'm carrying contraband or have any concern about what may be found in my bag. In fact, it has been a long time since I've even been asked to open my bags. It's just that my less-than-perfect patience does not do well with disembarking from a long flight, rounding the final corner, and seeing another planeload of weary passengers pouring toward immigration in front of me.

When I hop off a plane, I have one goal in mind: to pass as many straggling, wandering, and dithering people as possible and take the shortest route through the necessary processes to walk out those exit doors and breathe in the fresh air. Any flying companions I've ever had can humorously retell stories about my single-minded mission as I walk ahead of everybody else. (I know I fail the fruit-of-the-Spirit test here, so please, no sermons!)

But in the twenty-first century, it seems that electronic "smart gates" are the new world order. You simply scan your passport, answer a few questions, press a couple of buttons, look up at an automated camera, and watch it flash. Then glass gates give you access and away you go! Now, that's my kind of speed.

Access is king. It is crucial in so many different ways. Most of us in the Western world are grateful to have access to clean drinking water, medical care, and churches we can enter freely. Maybe you carry a key ring filled with keys that give you access to your home, car, workplace, post-office box, or safe—keys that give you access to a full and effective life.

What if I told you that you also have access to more of life, more of the kingdom of God, more of the love, joy, peace, blessing, radiance, and grace that define living in His will? This access is not something you need to fight for, something you line up for, or something that requires you to fill out forms or renew every five years. No, the Word of God says it plainly: "Through Him we both have access by one Spirit to the Father" (Ephesians 2:18). The "Him" is Jesus, the Son of God. And what do we know about the Father? Let me tell you.

He is all knowing, ever present, and available at every turn. He is love and light and hope and joy. In Him is strength when you feel weakest, answers to your deepest questions, and fullness to your life. His power is constantly at work within you, and He is able to do more—immeasurably more—than you can ask, think, or imagine. And the best part is that He is readily accessible with the keys to your abundant life and the blueprints of your daily needs, and He is poised with a stamp of favor for wherever you are going. He is always waiting with more in store.

Alive with Access

Do you feel as though you have access to everything God is doing? Is your spiritual life energetic and vibrant each and every morning that you wake, or do you find yourself physically present but spiritually decelerating? Are you spiritually alive or simply staying alive? Now that we're nearing the end of this book and have sought to unwrap some of the mysteries of journeying with God, can you honestly say that you are actively seeking out the heights and depths of His plans for your future? Or are you coasting through, content to simply exist, believing that your current reality is all God has? Are you hoping for more but not actively praying and looking for it?

When God breathed life into Adam, the man became both physically and spiritually alive. If the same hasn't already happened to you, it will happen to you the day Christ forgives your sins and you enter into the family of God. Your story of spiritual life begins that day, and if you are anything like the "baby Christians" I come in contact with, you will vibrate with new life and hope and excitement for the road ahead.

Or perhaps time has stolen some of your fervor. Maybe you would say that your passion has waned. If it took lining up to get into church, would you still stand in the cold, just to find out that you missed out on one service and need to wait for the next? I never want to forget the fact that I am the recipient of the greatest gift ever to be given on the planet. I want my passion to reflect that I am the carrier of the best news that humanity has ever received, that I am the mouthpiece of His message here and now.

But I would like to point out to you that spiritual life and spiritual activity are not the same thing. Growing up, I went to a church that can be described only as Pentecostal on steroids. My church was full of passion. I can still picture a handful of these passionate people who are forever immortalized in my childhood memories.

Everyone was labeled either "Brother" or "Sister," though I've changed their names in this book to protect their identities. Take Brother Klein, for example. He was at the door, greeting people, every Sunday. Brother Klein owned that space, and he made good and sure that it was his space and only his. Brother Pillsbury was another, probably one of the most encouraging old men you would ever meet. His demeanor was soft and his eyes were kind as he gave a playful punch to my shoulder and spoke words of life every time I passed by him as a young boy. Then there were Brother Morton and Brother Milner—good men as I remember them, dependable and solid. Brother Dejong was a father of eight, and the eldest of his sons is still one of my closest friends to this day, pastoring a thriving church in New Zealand.

Then there were the women. First of all, I think of Sister Jenkins. She was a spirited lady with a permanent seat on the second row to the left of the center aisle. Each time the preacher would stray into the aisle, preaching in an overly enthused and animated manner, she would be ready with a candy to hand him as he passed by. Granny Ethel sang in a voice that shook the entire auditorium and was always one full stanza in front of everyone else, enabling her to fill the space with her rather shrill voice. She was tiny in stature, but you always knew when she was in church!

Sister Paterson would dance and shake so violently during worship that the pews and rows around her seemed to vibrate in agreement.

Fervency was on a whole other level in this church. I could tell you stories for days of some of the crazy things I witnessed. I have a lot of good memories about my childhood church, but I sure want to lead something different today.

The thing about that environment, though, is that it was filled with spiritual activity—humming with spiritual talk and religious practice—but behind the scenes, there were defeated congregants, backbiting, gossip, and stale mentalities.

Spiritual activity is just not the same as spiritual life.

When I think about a church that is spiritually alive, I think about a place that is vibrant, faith filled, and grace filled. Where lost people are welcomed home, regardless of age, race, social status, or any other defining factors. A church that is focused on Jesus, continuously relying on the unmatchable power in His name and the hope He offers to everyone. A church that is spiritually alive and so obviously loves God, loves people, and loves life—not just on Sundays or during church events but out of the overflow of love, continually working and focusing on the Great Commission, wherever needed, at whatever cost. A church that pays attention to that which is pure and noble and is actively working to curb the ugliness of gossip and discontent within the body of Christ. A church that is focused on healthy community, relationship, and fellowship, where grace always takes precedence over law and works.

When I think about people who are spiritually alive, I think about those with zeal for their faith. When I think about the spirit of the people in the church I aspire to pastor, I think of people who are youthful in spirit, generous at heart, faith filled in confession, loving in nature, and inclusive in expression. Spiritually alive people recognize their need of God and their reliance on the Holy Spirit to guide, instruct, and sustain everything they do. That's why we have the following Scripture text:

No one's ever seen or heard anything like this,
Never so much as imagined anything quite like it—
What God has arranged for those who love him.

But *you've* seen and heard it because God by his Spirit has brought it all out into the open before you.

The Spirit, not content to flit around on the surface, dives into the depths of God, and brings out what God planned all along. Who ever knows what you're thinking and planning except you yourself? The same with God—except that he not only knows what he's thinking, but he lets *us* in on it. God offers a full report on the gifts of life and salvation that he is giving us. We don't have to rely on the world's guesses and opinions. We didn't learn this by reading books or going to school; we learned it from God, who taught us person-to-person through Jesus, and we're passing it on to you in the same firsthand, personal way.

The unspiritual self, just as it is by nature, can't receive the gifts of God's Spirit. There's no capacity for them. They seem like so much silliness. Spirit can be known only by spirit—God's Spirit and our spirits in open communion. Spiritually alive, we have access to everything God's Spirit is doing, and can't be judged by unspiritual critics. (1 Corinthians 2:9–16, MSG)

If I can leave you with one thing as we prepare to part ways in this penultimate chapter of *There Is More,* I pray that you would seek spiritual life. Let's heed the above words of Paul, which encourage us that it is when we are spiritually alive (alert, active, enthusiastic, and moving forward) that we have access to everything—yes, *everything*—God's Spirit is doing.

Learn from Apollos

Apollos was an Egyptian from Alexandria, a city that sits at the mouth of the Nile River. He lived at the time of Paul, serving Christ as an apostle. Apollos's upbringing in Alexandria was the training ground for the gift of rhetoric and oratory for which he was known. Alexandria was a center of education and learning, said to have had a library filled with around four hundred thousand volumes. The city was founded by Alexander the Great, who desired that it be an intellectual epicenter where Greek language, culture, and philosophy were not only celebrated but also debated in an effort to change the mind-sets of the masses.

Our first encounter with Apollos is recorded in the book of Acts, and I believe we can learn much from the life of this man who was so obviously spiritually alive:

A certain Jew named Apollos, born at Alexandria, an eloquent
man and mighty in the Scriptures, came to Ephesus. This man
had been instructed in the way of the Lord; and being fervent
in spirit, he spoke and taught accurately the things of the Lord,
though he knew only the baptism of John. So he began to speak

boldly in the synagogue. When Aquila and Priscilla heard him, they took him aside and explained to him the way of God more accurately. And when he desired to cross to Achaia, the brethren wrote, exhorting the disciples to receive him; and when he arrived, he greatly helped those who had believed through grace; for he vigorously refuted the Jews publicly, showing from the Scriptures that Jesus is the Christ. (18:24–28)

Hear this: Apollos was mighty in the Scriptures. I wonder if you or I could be described as "mighty in the Scriptures"? You might know the Word of God, but are you growing in it? Are you discovering new things, digging into the endless well that is the Bible, and searching the truth for application to your life? Reading the Word is imperative for your journey. It is without a doubt the next step, if you have not already made it your daily habit. All that God longs to tell you, show you, and teach you about the fulfilling life you are meant to live is hidden within this sacred text.

Throughout our time together, I've done my best to read with you some familiar stories and unearth other Scriptures in hope that it might teach and enlighten you and give you new perspective on timeless words. Fire has a tendency to go out unless it's fueled, and the way to fan the flame of the Spirit within you is to listen to the God-breathed words of your heavenly Father.

Deuteronomy 29:29 says, "The secret things belong to the LORD our God, but the things revealed belong to us and to our sons forever, that we may observe all the words of this law" (NASB). Do you want to know all that has been revealed? Like Apollos, become mighty in the Word.

This Alexandrian teacher of the Word was also fervent in spirit. I love being around passionate people—people such as Anthony, an inspirational young man who works for me in our California office. It seems that every time Anthony crosses my path, he greets me by declaring, "What a day!" At first when I heard this repeated anthem, I would laugh at his zeal because I've heard him say it on the best and worst, the coldest and warmest, and the easiest and most difficult of days. Is it simply hype, or does it ring true for Anthony? I think he really does love life and endeavors to find the best in each and every day. It's who he is, and it's contagious.

Then there's Lee, who I mentioned in chapter 9. Ask Lee how he is, and his stock answer is "I'm living the dream." He is known for that statement, and I think he may have spoken it into existence, as I see him excelling at everything he puts his hand to.

People who are alive in Christ are contagious, and when you live that way, your service of King Jesus can develop within you a fervency that draws people to the message that we together are all about. Imagine a church that is on fire for God. Picture crowds of people who throng to His house every Sunday and never want to leave. Imagine a fiery enthusiasm among your family and friends for the love of God and the outpouring of the Holy Spirit. Romans 12:11 implores us, "Never be lacking in zeal, but keep your spiritual fervor, serving the Lord" (NIVII).

Now, we've already covered the characteristic of authenticity and the necessity to live in a purehearted and open way, so I'm not talking about faking this kind of enthusiasm and putting on a happy face day in and day out simply to prove yourself a worthy servant of the Lord. There is something beautiful about living with passion even amid disappointment or sorrow. I have great respect for people who look for hope in heartbreak and can find a flicker of light in even the darkest of circumstances. That's what walking with the Lord does. That's what deep relationship, trust in His promises, and an understanding of "spiritual fervor" means.

God's love should compel us to serve Him with gladness. The gift of redemption we have received should bubble over inside us like a well-spring of passion and dedication to follow Jesus with our whole lives. But don't have one without the other. Apollos was growing in not only the *Word* of the Lord but also the *way* of the Lord. Acts 18:25 says, "He was well-educated in the way of the Master" (MSG). Too many people know the *Word* but not the *way* of the Lord.

What's the difference between Jesus's Word and His way? Have you ever thought about that? Over the years, I've come across many people who are strong in the Word and can expound on the context of Scripture, all the while cross-referencing it to other passages. But sadly, some who know the words so well are weak on the way of the Master by means of the fruit of the Spirit—the grace that Jesus displayed to broken and hurting people. Have you ever met anyone who is proud of his or her knowledge or theological expertise and qualifications but displays an angry, mean spirit to others? Is such a person spiritually alive? I'm not so sure.

Such people need a desire to live in the ways of the Lord and not just His Word. That's the attitude reflected in Psalm 25:4–5:

Show me your ways, O LORD;
Teach me Your paths.
Lead me in Your truth and teach me,
For You are the God of my salvation;
On You I wait all the day.

In contrast, have you ever met someone who is fervent in spirit but lacking a sound foundation in the Word? The Bible says that Apollos not only spoke with fervency but was also accurate in his teaching. Be confident *and* be accurate. Don't dilute the Word of truth with a lack of truth. If you are a seasoned Christian, devote yourself to continually learning and leaning in to teaching that will not only build your life but also allow you to build the lives of others.

I love that the Bible also gives weight to Apollo's gifting. From one scripture, we know he was not only a learned man but also "an eloquent speaker" (Acts 18:24, NLT). Apollos was flourishing in his gift and using it to glorify God.

You will never lose by attaching your gift to the purposes of God. What is it that you do? Are you in school? At home with young children? Building a business? Leading a ministry? Perhaps you are an empty nester, unsure of the next steps to take. Well, what does tomorrow look like? Who will you encounter, and what can you bring to the table?

Apollos followed Christ. He loved the things that Jesus loved and spent his life pursuing them. Just as Apollos did, you can take what is in your hand and use it to fulfill what is in your heart. Are you using your gifts for the glory of God? Your God-given gifts won't be fully realized unless you use them for God Himself.

A Work in Progress

If you really think about it, our growth is ongoing. Spiritual life is a journey, not a destination. Acts 18:25 records that "Apollos was accurate in everything he taught about Jesus *up to a point*" (MSG). He was mighty in the Word but still had a lot to learn. He was accurate . . . to a point. At what stage has your spiritual life stalled?

We can get stuck in a rhythm: turn up for church every Sunday, sit in the same seat, and speak to the same people. It's easy to say all the right things and act in all the right ways but lack any kind of growth in our spiritual selves. What point are you at? Don't stop now—God has so much more.

To be spiritually alive means being a constant seeker—searching out the ways of God and walking in them. Think about that for a moment. His ways are to love the hurting, preach the kingdom, and build the church. Jesus loved the Father, the lost, the poor, the world, and the church. If you are feeling stalled in momentum or as though you have reached the point at which you can go no further, seek out the things Jesus loved.

The apostle John wrote, "Anyone who claims to be intimate with God ought to live the same kind of life Jesus lived" (1 John 2:6, MSG). As followers of Christ, we are participating in the life of Jesus *even now*. And the way in which we engage in our lives, even the parts that are works in progress, matters greatly.

Don't allow any personal inadequacies to hold you back from forging ahead. Don't underestimate what the Spirit of God can do in you when you seek to learn and follow in His ways.

Humble and Bold

Enter Priscilla and Aquila, the others mentioned by name in Acts 18. "Apollos was accurate in everything he taught about Jesus up to a point, but he only went as far as the baptism of John. He preached with power in the meeting place. When Priscilla and Aquila heard him, they took him aside and told him the rest of the story" (18:25–26, MSG).

Have you ever stopped to wonder what that means? Who were these two, and what did they say? The significance of this relationship goes well beyond what one line indicates. Priscilla and Aquila were artisan-class citizens. They were tentmakers, humble in trade, of Jewish descent and likely pastoral in their practice, volunteering within the church.

What strikes me most about this relationship between them and Apollos is the humility of this eloquent Alexandrian and his readiness to receive counsel from tentmakers. He had probably sat at the feet of great scholars in Alexandria, yet he allowed simple tradespeople to correct his preaching in Ephesus. Readiness to receive is critical to our spiritual growth. Our ability to accept correction, to hear teaching and be challenged in our thinking, shows great humility and receptivity:

> A man's pride will bring him low,
> But a humble spirit will obtain honor.
> (Proverbs 29:23, NASB)

In the same way, notice how Priscilla and Aquila confronted Apollos. The Bible says, "They took him aside." They didn't go on social media. They didn't criticize or condemn him or heckle him in the public square. They didn't try to embarrass him or impress him with their own knowledge. Their approach was about honor.

I believe we can all learn something from their ways. Too often, in a day of instant gratification and "quick news," I have watched great men and women, with large platforms, embarrass themselves by lacking humility in their responses to people who think differently than they do.

Yes, there are many people who are mean spirited in their approach, but there are also multitudes with genuine questions and many people we can learn from if we would only humble ourselves to listen. All of us are on a learning journey. The moment we think we are right and everyone else is wrong, we are walking on dangerous ground.

Tom Wright, one of the leading New Testament scholars in the world today, once said that 20 percent of what he was teaching was wrong—he just didn't know which 20 percent it was!* None of us are beyond the point of learning, and that's why we are better together. God created community for a purpose, so let's lean in and learn from one another. No one has all the answers, and no one has a lock on the truth. We must be humble enough that our inadequacies will not stop us from growing and learning and stepping into the more that awaits.

Strap On Your Tank

What comes to mind when you think of the depths? How many times have you swum on the surface of the ocean and thought about all that is below?

A number of years ago, I had the privilege of going diving on the Great Barrier Reef. It was difficult to see from the surface exactly what was below, but after I descended into the depths of water, the radiance, colors, sheer beauty, and endless marine life were all a sight to behold. I've never seen anything quite like it.

There is so much more beneath the waves of the ocean than our eyes could ever see, and the same is true of our spiritual lives, our walks with

---

* David Wenham, review of Tom Wright's "Justification: God's Plan and Paul's Vision," *Evangelical Quarterly* 82, no. 3 (July 2010): 258–66.

God, and our glorious futures. "The Spirit, not content to flit around on the surface," wrote the apostle Paul, "dives into the depths of God, and brings out what God planned all along" (1 Corinthians 2:10, MSG). I *love* that thought!

Are you diving into the depths of God? Are you searching out the vast expanse of His never-ending kindness and love? Are you exploring the uninhabited places and hidden treasures that are far beneath the surface of His mercy and grace? As deep as the ocean is wide, so is His love for you, and so are His expansive plans for your life. Do you believe it? Are you teeming with life and hope, spiritually alive on the inside, or are you simply staying alive?

In a movie called *The Shallows,* a young lady named Nancy finds herself surfing on a deserted beach, enjoying the scenery of a faraway land. Out of nowhere, the unthinkable happens as she is bitten by a great white shark and struggles to hold on to her board and fight off the unexpected intruder. Wounded and alone, she clings to a rock, desperate to survive.

Too many Christians are like that: just spiritually surviving. They've been wounded and offended, perhaps wronged or misjudged, and instead of diving into the depths, they find themselves on the surface, finding respite from their wounds.

There is no denying it: spiritual wounds hurt. They are often deep and devastating, bringing with them the infections of doubt and despair. But we mustn't allow spiritual wounds to bring spiritual death. No disappointment this side of heaven should keep us from the richness of life in all its fullness.

Who do you need to forgive in order to move forward? What mindsets do you need to change, and which thoughts do you need to rebuke?

What ungodly or inadequate words have been spoken over your life that you need to leave on the surface so you can go deeper and discover the more that is waiting for you?

First Corinthians 2:9–10 says,

As it is written:

> Eye has not seen, nor ear heard,
> Nor have entered into the heart of man
> The things which God has prepared for those who
>   love Him.

But God has revealed them to us through His Spirit. For the Spirit searches all things, yes, *the deep things of God*.

As if echoing these verses, preacher and author Max Lucado wrote, "God's love has a width, length, height, and depth, but we will never reach the end of it. Our capacity to experience God's love will be exhausted and full long before God's capacity to give it is strained."[†]

Are you spiritually existing, or are you spiritually alive—not content to flit around on the surface, no longer comfortable to simply observe the things of God, but desperate to dive into the depths of all that awaits?

Just as there is more to the ocean floor than we can ever imagine—caverns of beauty and wonder, submerged mountains of passion and fury, undiscovered species, immovable boulders of truth beneath the waves—we will never reach the depths of all that God is. We will never find an end to the wonders of God—the facets of His thoughts and the

---

† Max Lucado, *Book of Ephesians: Where You Belong*, Life Lessons Series (Nashville: Thomas Nelson, 2006), 59.

ways of His hand. There is more of Him and more to know than we can ask, think, or even imagine. Immeasurably more.

Strap on your tank, dear friend. Get yourself ready and He will prove Himself faithful. Prepare for the dive, get ready to go deeper, and decide that what you want is all He has and more.

Epilogue

There Is More

As I mentioned in chapter 13, it's a moment I always enjoy on a certain Sunday night annually in February when we gather our entire church—every service, location, and campus around the globe—and share the vision for where God is leading us as a family in the new year. "Drumroll, please"—that's the sense of expectancy about the more of the future we all have on these occasions.

As I sit and write this, the memory is fresh because it was a mere twelve hours ago that we gathered in every Australian location and linked to share with our church family the exciting new endeavors and cities that God had placed on our hearts and in our paths. At this very moment, Hillsong Church Phoenix and Hillsong Church Los Angeles are preparing for their Sunday services—the last of the "rooms" to roll out Vision Sunday around the world. It takes a full thirty hours from the beginning of the first Sunday morning service in Sydney until the end of the last Sunday night service in Los Angeles.

Bobbie often refers to Hillsong Church globally as "one house, many rooms." She tells a story about the day the Lord dropped that phrase in her spirit after driving away from our first-ever gathering at Hillsong New York City. We had a sensitivity for this city and new church plant because building in Manhattan also meant we were losing our older son to a dream he had held on to for many years—a dream to one day link with his Bible college buddy Carl Lentz and plant a church in New York City. As Bobbie recalls the vision, she saw a stunning, expansive mansion with many windows—the kind you might imagine is being prepared in heaven (see John 14:2–3)—and felt the Lord say in context of this new plant, "You've just added another room to this glorious house that is being built. Nothing is being lost, only gained." The language of "one house, many rooms" stems from this vision and revelation.

As a now far-reaching, diverse, and beautiful global church, Hillsong remains united. We are one house, one heart, one vision, serving a world in need through countless "rooms" and congregations around the world but all under the banner of Jesus Christ.

I tell you all this because it still causes me to shake my head in disbelief, still leads me to this place where I find myself—on a Monday morning in my lounge room—awed at what just took place. Rewind to last night's gathering as we shared with our church that this year would see adding not only one room but three! Hillsong Church Portugal, Hillsong Church San Francisco, and Hillsong Church Israel were about to be birthed by the right people, in the right cities, at the right time. Even as I type these words, I am catching my breath a little at the enormity of the task ahead and the gratitude I feel for the opportunities we have: another church on European shores, a church in a city that is leading the world in development of technology and innovation, and a church in the Middle East! And even among all these announcements, there was so much more to say about everything that the Lord was doing among His people and His church. Isn't that just the nature of God?

Perhaps in a world as fast paced and far reaching as this one, these prospects don't surprise you. But let me remind you of the first chapter of this book, where I introduced you to my seventeen-year-old self: shy and stuttering, a pastor's son from government housing in the small nation of New Zealand with nothing but a dream in his heart. I don't tell you all this with the hope that you might be impressed by any achievements of ours but rather to encourage you that when God takes our less and adds His blessing, favor, power, and purpose, the results are more than you could ever dare to imagine.

I want to use our last few moments together to remind you again that you were born for a purpose bigger than you could ever accomplish on your own. That you are destined for greatness and have all the tools at your disposal to pick up and carve out a path ahead of fruitfulness with the God of the universe on your side—a God who isn't afraid of our mess and who delights in our happiness and bends low in our weakness. He is ever present and so capable to not only make all things new but make something out of nothing. He is the kind of God who defies all odds and goes the distance to enable you to reach your potential and discover a life of abundance, both now and forever. All He needs is your heart, your willingness, and your commitment to the cause.

The kingdom of God *is* advancing on the earth in unprecedented ways, and I don't know about you, but I want to be a part of the army that is rising up and declaring to the nations that there is so much more to life than what we have already seen.

No matter what you have experienced or are experiencing, I want to say to you:

On the other side of this triumph, there is *more.*

On the other side of that failure, there is *more.*

On the other side of this sickness, there is *more.*

On the other side of your mountain, there is *more.*

On the other side of this heartache, there is *more.*

On the other side of this earth, there is so much *more.*

Ephesians 3 is not some insignificant passage hidden inside a large sacred text. We know that every word of the Bible is divinely inspired and infused with truth and power for our edification and help—a gift that God trusts us not only to unwrap but also to steward and live out. The promise that is embedded within this chapter daily causes me to lift my eyes higher and dream bigger and go deeper into the unending capacity of the one who saved me and set me free:

God's love is meteoric,
    his loyalty astronomic,
His purpose titanic,
    his verdicts oceanic.
Yet in his largeness
    nothing gets lost;
Not a man, not a mouse,
    slips through the cracks. (Psalm 36:5–6, MSG)

Nothing gets lost. If you feel unsure or unsteady, lost or overlooked, or you simply need to be reminded again, let me be the one to do that.

He sees you. He knows you (better than you could know yourself), and He waits with open arms, available with anything you need. At the beginning of this book, I quoted the young English orphan Oliver Twist, who was forlorn and longed for just a little bit more. Let me assure you that you are no longer an orphan but are adopted into the family of God and an heir to an unending throne and an inheritance that will outlast space and time. Your portion is exceedingly abundantly above anything you can think, ask, or imagine.

There is so much more I could say. I can't begin to explain or unravel all that is ahead of you or fathom all that God has planned. This book can barely touch on the unending nature of all He is. But this I do know: I'm going to live all my days to serve Him. I'm going to give all my capability to build that which He loves: His church. I'm going to seek His face and open myself up to His leading and promises every day of my life. I pray that you will too.

So, here's the challenge. Live with expectancy. Steep yourself in God's promises and travel the road of obedience to Christ with your eyes wide open to every facet of His faithfulness. Make *more* room for others, make *more* space for God, and watch Him make *more* of your dreams—the ones you dared to pray and the ones you never have—come to life.

Thank you for the privilege of speaking into your life in this season as you have read this book. I pray that as you turn the last page of this final chapter, you will feel encouraged and victorious—that you will be more aware of God's deep love for you and the adventure that is life with Christ. There is immeasurable potential within—plans and purposes beyond your wildest dreams. Let that sink in and allow me to speak these words over you as a prayer and benediction from someone who has experienced the more of God and continues to be blown away by the enormity of His promises and faithfulness:

> Now to Him who is able to do exceedingly abundantly above all that we ask or think, according to the power that works in us, to Him be glory in the church by Christ Jesus to all generations, forever and ever. Amen.

ACKNOWLEDGMENTS

I have invested my heart and soul into *Live Love Lead* and now this book, *There Is More*. But I want to give special mention to Karalee Fielding, a beautiful young wife and mum who is just as passionate about these projects and has been there with me through every step of the process. Despite being pregnant and enduring a season of serious morning sickness while we wrote this book, as well as navigating both her and my international travel, she managed to keep the process going and always meet my deadlines along the way. Ben Fielding (for your long suffering) and Karalee, what gifts you are to Bobbie and me.

ABOUT THE AUTHOR

Brian Houston is an international bestselling author and the global senior pastor of Hillsong Church, a family of congregations comprising more than one hundred thousand weekly attendees. Considered by many to be a leading voice in the shaping of contemporary leadership values and church culture, Pastor Brian is highly regarded for his bold innovation and passion for the local church.

Brian's infectious love for people and his empowering brand of leadership reaches millions of people weekly through his program, *Brian Houston TV,* and draws tens of thousands annually to Hillsong Conference in Sydney, London, and the USA. He is also the president of the recently launched Hillsong Channel, president of Hillsong College, and the executive producer of countless gold and platinum albums that have come from the Hillsong worship team.

Brian and his wife, Bobbie, have three grown children and live in Sydney, Australia, and Orange County, California